Coping with
Sexual Relationships

Dr Judy Bury, the General Editor of this series, has worked in general practice and family planning for many years. She writes regularly on medical topics, and has a particular interest in self-help approaches to health care.

Other titles in the series include

*Coping with Caesarean and
other difficult births*

Coping with Aging Parents

Coping with a Dying Relative

Coping with Sexual Relationships

Coping with Skin and Hair Problems

Coping with Periods

Coping with Sexual Relationships

Judy Greenwood

WITH A FOREWORD BY
Professor Anthony Clare

MACDONALD PUBLISHERS
EDINBURGH

IN ASSOCIATION WITH CHANNEL FOUR TELEVISION COMPANY AND
YORKSHIRE TELEVISION LIMITED

© Judy Greenwood, 1984

ISBN 0 86334 043 1 (Hardback)
ISBN 0 86334 042 3 (Paperback)

Published by
Macdonald Publishers, Edinburgh
Edgefield Road, Loanhead,
Midlothian EH20 9SY

Design and cover by Iain McKinlay
Illustrations by Jo Hignett
Series editor Judy Bury

Printed in Scotland by
Macdonald Printers (Edinburgh) Limited
Edgefield Road, Loanhead, Midlothian

Contents

Dedication

To Mollie and Albert, who taught me all I need to know about love and affection; John, who helped put it into practice; Sophie, Tom and Phil, who confirm and continue the process— and The Medical Secs. and Betty, who kindly put it into print.

Foreword

In a world apparently awash with sexual imagery, erotic stimuli and frank speaking, a book on how to cope with intimate relationships might appear somewhat redundant. Yet it is becoming readily apparent that much of what is written about human sexuality, particularly by self-nominated sex experts, is mechanistic and reductionist and transforms the most personal and self-revealing of human acts into little more than a gymnastic feat. In the words of one of sex education's severest critics, Thomas Szasz, having a good orgasm becomes akin to having a good bowel movement.

This book, however, refrains from treating sexual actions and reactions as merely genital. Dr Greenwood has written a book which is first and foremost about personal relationships and is itself a personal view culled from experience as a counsellor, confidante and friend. The heightened expectations, provoked by mass media and the apparent permissive ideology of our time, are acknowledged. So too is the danger of medicalising sexual difficulties and variations into diseases to be treated by suitably qualified experts. Dr Greenwood's intention is to draw the attention of her readers to the immense diversity and variety in sexual relationships, the ubiquity of sexual set-backs and short-comings and the opportunities for sexual development and harmony. Information is provided with the minimum of moralising and the maximum of accuracy. This book may not eliminate sexual difficulties but it will go some way towards reducing misunderstanding and tensions. It may seem a modest aim but given the unrealistic hyperbole concerning sexual fulfilment and the Calvinistic forebodings expressed by critics of the permissive society, its moderation is its strength and its justification.

Anthony Clare
London, February 1984

Introduction

This book has been deliberately kept short in the hope that you will read it all. I have tried to include many of the everyday problems I see when working with ordinary couples. These are people like you and me who are trying to establish or maintain a close physical and emotional relationship with another person in the difficult social climate of the 80s.

Today we expect more from ourselves, from sex and from our relationships than ever before. The mass media and the 'permissive society' have increased our self-awareness and our expectations from sexual relationships, at the same time that social mobility and increased work opportunities for women have decreased our family networks and community contacts. We now focus most of these increased expectations on the intimacy of one close relationship. But both men and women are also demanding more freedom for 'personal growth' whilst in this close relationship, and it is the pressure from these increased levels of expectation—both for relationships and for self-development—that seem to have led to the high incidence of marital breakdown and the increase in those seeking help with sexual problems. Undoubtedly, too, women's increased assertiveness and freedom from total dependence on their partner has meant that marriages previously 'tolerated' are now acknowledged as failures and this has also added to the rising divorce statistics.

I hope that this book will make you question what you should realistically expect from your own close relationships, and perhaps help you sort out the minor sexual problems that can afflict anyone from time to time. It underlines the importance of understanding your own needs as well as those of your partner and trying to maintain a relaxed and tension-free emotional climate between you if sex is to flourish. Such a climate can only be achieved by good communication, the controlled airing of grievances, a general air of goodwill and the desire to succeed. Lasting sexual relationships do not survive by chance, but rather by regular servicing and regular adjustments to accommodate the changing circumstances and needs of each partner over a lifetime. I hope that the contents of this book may help you to adjust more sensitively to your own sex life and perhaps to understand better the everyday problems of those close to you.

Judy Greenwood,
Edinburgh, 1983

1 Uses and Abuses of Sex

The aim of this book is *not* to provide a comprehensive account of all forms of sexual behaviour and problems, but rather to examine the common pitfalls of everyday sexual relationships and what you can do about them.

We all have the capacity to respond sexually—it is an intrinsic function of our adult body—but how we choose to make use of this function depends on many complex factors, such as the attitudes and values about sex we have acquired in our upbringing, the cultural atmosphere in which we live, and of course the changing circumstances of our close relationships. In fact, coming to terms with our sexuality is a very fundamental part of maturing. For some, this process occurs smoothly and naturally; for others, the acceptance of anything remotely related to sex remains painfully unresolved or distorted throughout adulthood, leading to problems in personal relationships, or in some cases a total avoidance of intimacy altogether. Even if we have come to terms with being a sexual person, we may use our sexuality in a variety of differing ways over a lifetime. So may our partner—and here's the rub! He may be using sex for a very different reason from the one I'm using it for.

Whether or not sexual behaviour was simply designed for procreation alone—as some would have us believe—in this modern world it serves a diversity of functions. We should be aware of these if we are to avoid the confusions and hurts that may arise from misunderstanding our sexual experiences.

Let us begin by looking at some of the more positive uses of sexuality and sexual behaviour, which we tend to lump together as that emotive word 'sex'.

Uses of sex

Pleasure

During childhood, body sensations form an important part of life's pleasures and stimulation. We particularly enjoy the oral experience of sucking—breast, bottle, thumb, toys and later progressing to lollipops and eventually on to kissing (some also risk their lives with pipes and cigarettes). Our body give us sensual delights too—being held and cuddled, tickled, roly-polying down a hill, stroking a furry animal, running about without clothes on a hot day and squealing with delight and abandonment. We also enjoy the proximity and intimacy of cuddling, of wrestling, and rough-and-tumble play. If we are lucky, as adults we can recapture such 'innocent' joy in the sensuality of our body with sexual pleasure—whether alone by stimulating ourselves, or with the added bonus of intimacy with another person.

Sexual pleasure is not only a fleeting experience of the moment, but often acts as a natural relaxant—releasing the tensions of the day and thus improving our emotional and physical well-being over a considerable period of time. Most teenagers, especially boys at the height of their sexual drive, masturbate regularly and it is sad that the pleasure and release derived from such harmless behaviour is often masked by guilt and anxiety about the possible harm they fear they are doing to themselves—anxiety they feel unable to share with anyone.

In marriage, one partner may attach significantly more importance to sexual pleasure than the other, and this can cause conflict. A negotiated settlement of an acceptable minimum of joint sexual activity may be necessary with the agreement that the more 'sensual' partner may need to look after him- or herself on occasions. Masturbation within marriage is common and need not be a problem unless it produces resentment, or interferes with the couple's shared sexual relationship. By mutual choice, it is often kept secret from the other partner.

To confirm our 'gender'

Before puberty, boys and girls are physically more similar and, as a result, less aware of gender differences. But, once through puberty, our so-called 'secondary sexual characteristics'—breasts, altered body shape and voice, changed genitals and altered physiology—make us more conscious of which sex we actually are. Not only do we *feel* different, but we are *treated* differently by the opposite sex—a new tension is in the air, making us even more conscious of our *femininity* or *masculinity* (or painfully aware of the lack of it!).

A common problem after puberty is anorexia—that complex complaint which predominantly affects girls and is sometimes triggered by their first awakening to a sense of femininity. The idea of facing the challenges of adult sexuality seems to overwhelm them and that, combined with a distorted sense of body-image and perhaps difficulties in family relationships, is enough to trigger the anorexic process—severe dieting, weight loss and amenorrhoea (the suspension of monthly periods once the weight has dropped below a critical level). Boys facing a similar crisis are more likely to become socially withdrawn and isolated (schizoid), although anorexia is occasionally seen in them too.

To bolster our self-esteem and sense of attractiveness

As mature adults, most of us try to maintain a precarious balancing act with our 'self-esteem' or sense of self-worth—between what *we* think of ourselves and what *others* think of us. If we are biased too much either way, our security becomes precarious. As youngsters we rarely get the balancing act right. Our concern about what others think of us may be paramount (it may not be parents—but certainly the gang we belong to), and especially our concern about what the opposite sex thinks about us (or our own, if we are homosexual).

Sexual attractiveness, or sex appeal, is an elusive quality—and fortunately has many facets, both in the eye of the beholder and the beheld. We all have a fantasy view of a 'perfect self' that we would *choose* to look like (usually a photo-fit combination of the best of a variety of famous people), and as a result we tend always to rate ourselves as 'less than perfect' on this personal yardstick. Despite this, we can still *feel* attractive if we are in the right setting and in the right mood. Feeling attractive is a combination of feeling accepted by another person and by oneself—and at the end of the day this rarely depends on looks alone!

But how do you persuade a physically handicapped young person to believe that, even though perfectly formed adults often feel ugly and unworthy of another's attention, he or she can feel attractive? Mercifully, personality and style can be as attractive as our external packaging and we all know some physically unappealing but sexually attractive people.

It is fascinating to ponder on the variations in standards of sexual attraction over the centuries—body shape, colour, disposition, weight, how fashions can change. Some people can feel attracted to people who look like themselves (assortative mating), others to polar opposites. Studies suggest that poorer people tend to marry people who live nearby, who are similar in 'attractiveness' and strengths to themselves, and come from similar home backgrounds; but as you climb the social ladder there is more scatter in the choice of partner. But remember—our choice of life-long partner may be based on very different criteria from our choice of whom we find sexually attractive; a whole book could be written on this subject in itself!

It would have been easier for all of us if sexual attractiveness switched off after we had chosen our mate—but nature didn't plan it that way. Presumably the advantages of remaining attractive to our partner outweigh the disadvantages of continuing to be attractive to and attracted by other people after marriage. Coming to terms with the 'siren-call' of extra-marital flirtations, by recognising them for what they are—superficial responses to novelty and packaging—allow most couples to continue to enjoy the short-term pleasure of such confidence-boosting behaviour without jeopardising their marriages. But it can be dangerous or hurtful if ill-controlled; so beware and be sensitive.

Intimacy

Mutually satisfying sexual intimacy between two adults usually promotes emotional bonding and a feeling of dependence on each other. A good sexual relationship can cement the intimacy of a marriage and hold it firm through the challenges of a lifetime. The sexual act itself implies exposing ourselves to vulnerability and hurt as well as to the physical and psychological pleasure of the shared experience. Our 'civil' defences are dropped as we discard our clothes and allow another person access to the secret and private parts of our body. We are emotionally and physically vulnerable and only if we trust our partner can we relax enough to abandon ourselves to the full pleasures of our shared sexual responses. Ridicule or betrayal of this secret part of a relationship may change the intimacy of the relationship for ever.

For some, intimacy is enhanced by the predictability and cosiness of a long and shared relationship; for others, intimacy is replaced by boredom as the marriage loses its sparkle. Some people cannot cope with intimacy at all (perhaps having been smothered by an overwhelming parent in childhood—or having grown up in an emotionally-deprived background). They separate sex from relationships, and can only relax with a stranger, or with casual or paid-for sex. Emotional proximity is too much to handle. Enforced sex or rape is the antithesis of intimacy and sometimes causes the victim to experience long-standing difficulties thereafter in associating sex with anything loving and shared.

Children

I have put this subject at the end of the 'uses of sex' list, although in the natural order of things it would have appeared first; but I believe the order we have presented here is perhaps the one we experience in our sexual development and unfolding.

Some people have argued that women who lose their sexual interest and appetite when using the contraceptive pill do so because they feel that lovemaking is now too safe. They have lost the frisson of excitement that the risk of pregnancy gives to sex. How biological is our need to link sex with reproduction? No one really knows. Some religions see the two as inescapably linked, but we must remind ourselves that it has only been in the last fifty years that we have reliably been able to separate the two. A quick read through the agonised letters from ordinary women to Marie Stopes at the beginning of this century will quickly reveal how far we have come from the misery of recurrent and unwanted pregnancies, and the consequent subservience and dependence of women on men for their financial and social survival.

The fact that sex has been liberated from pregnancy can only be applauded—although new challenges have now arisen as a result, not least women's welcome freedom to dictate to their own bodies (and their menfolk?), a welcome reduction in birthrate (see Chapter 4), and a perhaps less welcome increase in the divorce rate.

Abuses of sex

Whereas most of the uses to which we put sex are fairly universally experienced, the personal abuses of sex are perhaps less common.

Nevertheless, many youngsters go through a stage where sexual expression is simply seen as a weapon of rebellion against adult authority, and a means of flouting conventions and rules, which takes little effort or expense on their part. In single-sex institutions, this may take the form of homosexual 'horse-play' which does no one any harm. But if the rebellion involves irresponsible sexual behaviour between boys and girls, then it is highly unlikely that at the same time they will be responsible enough to consider contraception, and the rebellion often ends by back-firing—with an unwanted pregnancy as the outcome.

Risk-taking

Most people experience a mixture of exhilaration, excitement and fear in their early sexual experiences which leads to a sense of heightened awareness. Who has forgotten their first kiss? But some people seem unable to mature from those early exhilarating experiences to feeling satisfied by the predictable and less titillating sexual lifestyle of a conventional marriage or long-term relationship. They crave the exhilaration of risk-taking, and may use sex as a means to achieve their goal—via extra-marital sex, forbidden sex such as paedophilia or worst of all, incest, which violates both the trust of an adult/child relationship and the taboos of sex within the family. There is little doubt that, once sex is released from conventional social controls, it becomes 'risky' and, by definition, to some more exhilarating, to others more threatening.

Within marriage, fighting sexual boredom may induce a couple to risk having sexual intercourse in a novel setting—in the countryside, in their car—where the risk of being found adds extra excitement to their well-rehearsed routine. Extra-marital sex, whether in fantasy or reality, is used by some as a means of restoring a jaded sexual appetite as much as procuring heightened responses; but this is a dangerous game, unless the emotions and circumstances of both parties are rigorously delineated and protected. People who think they can divorce their emotions from their genital responses often end up with a real divorce! I'll be looking at this subject again in Chapter 3.

Uses and Abuses of Sex

Sex used as an expression of anger

It is perhaps ironic that the same behaviour which can lead to intimacy and great bonds of affection and love, can also be evoked as an expression of anger and hostility. Rape is perhaps the ultimate act of hostility. It is usually an angry act of vengeance against women, rather than the frenzied expression of sexual frustration. So, too, exhibitionism—exposure of the penis—is usually to induce fear in a woman to make the man *feel* more powerful.

Women, too, can express their anger in sexual behaviour. Perhaps using more subtle techniques, they can metaphorically castrate their partner—fail to respond, ridicule or criticise his lovemaking, or flaunt their sexuality in a cruel and mocking way at a vulnerable and inexperienced man. Both men and women can withdraw sex from a relationship as an expression of anger—the ultimate weapon when resentment cannot be resolved by discussion (see Chapter 3).

Sex as power

Sexual favours can be used as a form of currency in distorted relationships. Some people exploit others' sexual dependence on them in a highly manipulative fashion. Mentally handicapped people are particularly vulnerable to sexual exploitation by the less handicapped, and this is one of the problems that faces our new ideology concerning their freedom to lead full and normal lives in the community.

Some unscrupulous women can sexually ensnare a man, then exploit his infatuation for financial gain or even blackmail. Men can exploit women and vice versa in prostitution. Within marriage many a partner, both male and female, will use sexual favours as a reward for acceptable behaviour from the spouse—which negates the whole concept of mutual sexual affection.

Commercial exploitation

We are continually bombarded, via the media, with expensive messages designed to override our biological common sense about sex and sexual attractiveness. The advertisers are no fools. They have discovered that our lack of sexual confidence is our 'Achilles Heel'—our most vulnerable facet, and probably the most likely pressure point to encourage us to part company with our money unwisely (second only to health). I have to say that the subtle promises of vodka, whisky, bath essence, cigars, perfume and hair-spray have all failed to materialise in *my* experience!

In conclusion: sex has many uses and abuses and, as a result, is open to much misinterpretation or conflicting messages. Two people may engage in the same sexual relationship for totally different reasons—each making mistaken assumptions about the other's motives or commitment. Attitudes and values concerning sexual expression may vary widely within the same person over a lifetime, and it is essential, in order to avoid misunderstandings and hurt, that people using or abusing sexual attraction and relationships are not only aware of their own motives, but can be honest with others who may otherwise be hurt by their deception.

2 Sexual Development

Coping with Sexual Relationships

It is only by understanding the processes of sexual development which most people go through at a variable age, that we can really make sense of the place of sexuality in our own adult lives. Our capacity to have sexual feelings—our sexuality—does not arise fully-fledged with the onset of puberty, but rather grows over a period of time. Important milestones like our first period, or first ejaculation, our first real kiss and first act of intercourse may cause our preoccupation with sex to become temporarily heightened, but I believe we do not reach full sexual maturity for many years after our first faltering step of sexual activity—if ever. By sexual maturity I mean being able to acknowledge and accept, without guilt feelings or anxiety, our own sexuality and sexual responses as a healthy and integral part of our personality; and being able to enjoy physical and emotional intimacy with another person in a relaxed, responsive and confident manner, while at the same time showing appropriate sensitivity and concern for the feelings and needs of the other person.

Our 'sexual unfolding', as it has been called, requires a series of complex readjustments to occur both in our view of ourself and our view of those close to us (usually our parents). Some of these changes happen almost unconsciously; others intrude painfully on our consciousness, making us feel awkward, insecure and unpleasantly self-aware.

● First there is our developing *sense of body awareness*: what sex we are (our gender), what shape we are (a theme that often continues to concern us throughout adult life), and what new processes are going on in our body.

● Then there are those subtle changes in the *focus of our affection and libido* (emotional drive) from being exclusively directed towards our parents in childhood, to our involvement and commitment to a group of close friends and perhaps, later, to the emotional investment in one key individual whose importance may supersede all past bonds and ties. This process may be upset—delayed or speeded up if our relationship with our parents seemed deficient or emotionally unfulfilling.

● In the course of this complex process, we are probably unaware that we are also defining our *sexual orientation*: do we feel more comfortable in the intimacy of same-sex relationships or with the opposite sex—are we homosexual or heterosexual, or somewhere in between? We may feel very anxious if we find ourselves homosexually inclined, because by now we will have incorporated society's attitudes and biases about homosexuality (see Chapter 6). Our sexual preferences may remain unstable for a considerable period of time, with bizarre fantasies about all manner of sexual relationships.

● Our first tentative steps towards *physical sexual expression* may come early or late in sexual development, depending on circumstances. We must learn to develop a realistic view about what we can expect from sexual activity, both alone and with another—trying to sort out facts from fantasies and old wives' tales.

● We must learn to question, and then re-process as an adult the *sexual inhibitions and taboos* acquired and accepted in childhood, if we are to be relaxed about our new-found sexuality.

● We must honestly acknowledge ourselves as being sexual creatures not only in secret, but in our interaction with others—maturely accepting this as something we choose to be involved in for intimacy and pleasure, rather than for reasons of rebellion or risk-taking.

● We must evolve a *personal sexual value system* that can cope with private decisions about such questions as masturbation, virginity, monogamy, promiscuity, extramarital sex and divorce. As we grapple with what we decide is the appropriate sexual responsibility for ourselves, and as our sexual confidence develops, we must also start to acquire a responsibility and sensitivity to the sexual needs of others, both in our own relationships and in the authority we may hold over others' behaviour—either our own children or those over whom we have control—ultimately learning to recognise our sexual responsibility towards society as a whole.

What a prospect! And what a good job we can get so much pleasure from sex as well! It is hardly surprising that some of us baulk at the beginning of the sexual journey, and see celibacy as an easier option.

Sexual development is currently taking place in a very different world from that of our forebears. It is hard to appreciate the massive shift in social attitudes which has occurred within one generation in the twentieth century. We now have freely available contraception, women's new assertiveness, increased personal expectations, sexual permissiveness and explicitness in films and TV, commercial exploitation of teenagers in music and fashion and sex, increased teenage alcohol and drug use, more social and geographical mobility, easier travel, and high rates of unemployment and divorce. A teenager's parents may be divorced—both from each other, and from any understanding of what it is like to grow up today.

Our sexual unfolding must also be seen in the context of the general changes in our lives as we pass from childhood. Psychiatrists use the expression 'adolescent tasks' to describe the challenges we must surmount to reach adulthood, but I firmly believe that these tasks continue to be important throughout life for a secure identity and self-confidence, without which a healthy sexual adjustment is less likely. They are:

The establishment and maintenance of *friends*

A recognisable *work-role*, hobby, sport or pastime on which we can hang a job-description for ourselves (I'm a . . .)

Maintaining an appropriate relationship with *parents* (see Chapter 5)

Comfort with our *body functions*

Emotional control

Sexual adjustment

Friends

Friends of the same age (a peer group) are particularly important in adolescence, as they make coping with our developing sexuality and early relationships so much easier. As we move from dependence on our parents' attitudes and values, we temporarily rely on the standards and advice of our close friends, before finally achieving adult autonomy and the confidence to make our own decisions about what we believe is right or wrong. Peer-group pressure to conform is strong, and adolescent trends are obvious for all to see—in clothes, hair, music and style. But kids still have big personal decisions to make despite the apparent conformity: am I a swinger or swot, a smoker or health freak, a conformer or rebel, sexy or chaste, assertive or passive? Even so, the reactions of friends make it easier to discover which role suits you best.

Close friends continue to play an important part in most adult lives too (for women more than for men), and having a trusted confidant with whom one can share the troubles of everyday existence, and with whom one can feel 'good' and accepted, often helps a marriage enormously. A spouse cannot be one's only friend, confidant and adviser because he or she is too emotionally involved—we need outside contacts too. A bored and lonely housewife can be transformed by joining a women's group, and her marriage and sex life is often transformed too.

Work

Unemployed youngsters and adults have many disadvantages: no hook on which to hang their identity, no money, no status, and fewer social contacts. Youngsters become trapped in the tensions of home and in a prolonged 'adolescence' beyond their time. They feel less attractive, and this low self-esteem may colour their developing sexuality. Some are able to establish good and rewarding relationships and fill their lives with intimacy and plan for the future; others simply see sex as a stepping stone to filling the work-identity vacuum with pregnancy (the status of motherhood gives a job description for the next sixteen years!), or the money vacuum with prostitution. Adults—particularly men—are similarly handicapped by unemployment. Their self-confidence lessens, tensions rise at home as roles become confused, and the sexual relationship may suffer as a result.

For the majority of youngsters who are at work, their type of work and status will govern their social life and perhaps their self-confidence. Sport and hobbies may fill the image gap for some, whether at work or not, and life outside work and home is undoubtedly important for the broad-based life of a secure teenager (and adult). Keeping a balance between time and energy for work, time for hobbies and sports—which might be seen as personal time—and time for relationships, parents, friends and sexual partner is far from easy. We can only learn by trial and error, and from judging whether our needs or their needs are more important. Many marriages founder when couples cannot get this fundamental juggling act right with each other. It may be during our early teenage relationships that we first recognise the difficulties of satisfying several demands on our time, with girl-friend, mother, teacher, friends, sport, all competing for our attention.

Accepting new body and new physiology

New body

No one is completely satisfied with the shape of his or her body, but adolescence is a peak time for such disappointments and anxieties to be felt. Height, weight, breasts, face, size and shape of genitals—as well as pimples and dandruff—are agonised over or compared unfavourably with others. Coming to terms with and accepting our new-look body needs mirrors, reassurance and sympathy. We need opportunities for experimentation with clothes, hair and personal style to get it right—not only for ourselves, but for the effect we have on others too. Adults should listen to adolescent anxieties sensitively and sympathetically. If they are honest they have many of the same problems too—and such sharing helps. Mid-life is another peak time for agonising over bodies, as the aging process begins to affect our shape, our fitness and our sexual attractiveness. In fact, these 'adolescent tasks' go on for ever!

New function

Youngsters should be warned about the changes of body functions *before* they happen. That way no one is caught unawares, and parental embarrassment can be kept to a minimum. It really is essential, and much easier, to talk about menstruation, wet dreams and erections *before* puberty.

Between the ages of ten and seventeen a girl will probably start her periods. She needs someone to share the mechanics of coping with this—sensible advice about the management of menstrual hygiene. Usually a combination of parents, sex education at school, and good leaflets or magazine articles is enough. Mothers may have less trouble talking about this, because it has nothing to do with sex and sexual responses. Fathers, on the other hand, have a more difficult task. It is impossible to discuss their son's body changes without talking about erections and wet dreams—both *very much* to do with sexual responses. As a result they tend not to broach the subject at all.

Spontaneous erections and nocturnal emissions (wet dreams) occur around adolescence in most boys (between about twelve and eighteen) and may cause great embarrassment or anxiety if not understood. Some young boys think they have bled or wet the bed when they have their first emission. About this time they learn that if they stimulate their own body they can produce an erection, feel sexually aroused and reach a climax. Most boys masturbate regularly and frequently. This is perfectly normal and harmless behaviour, but may cause anxiety because of guilt feelings, or fear that they have damaged themselves. Some boys experience quite florid fantasies when they masturbate and may have additional anxieties that they might become potential rapists or sadists (which is most unlikely).

Boys develop erections at the slightest emotional or physical stimulus in their teens, and this may lead to a fear of homosexuality if a spontaneous erection occurs during horseplay with another boy (see Chapter 6). It must be emphasised that there is an enormous difference between boys and girls early in adolescence—boys learn about their sexual responses as girls learn about menstruation and reproduction. This is not surprising at this stage, as boys' genitalia and sexual responses are more obvious. Boys are likely to fantasise about physical sexual experience, whilst girls are inclined to romantic fantasies. In the 1960s and 70s, with the advent of more permissive sexual attitudes, an increased proportion of girls began to masturbate and understand their responses, and many now use tampons, which means that they understand their anatomy better too.

Emotional control

As youngsters separate from their parents' control, they should acquire the skill of regulating their own emotions in order both to live comfortably with themselves and, perhaps, in the close proximity of a relationship with another person (when it is even more important to have emotional control). By control, I mean being able to identify, acknowledge and deal with the powerful emotions to which we are subject without their undermining our self-confidence or our relationships. We must learn to regulate depression, anxiety and anger. The regulation of anger is particularly important for relationships, and learning to express this constructively rather than destructively may take many years of practice.

Some people seem to drift from allowing parents to control their emotions to expecting their spouse to take over the same function. One often hears of a long-suffering husband trying to reassure his unduly anxious or pessimistic wife, just as her parents must have done in years gone by. How vulnerable she will be if he dies or leaves home, and what a strain she is putting on the marriage as a result! It is far better for people to learn a degree of emotional self-sufficiency before embarking on a sexual relationship, and especially on a long-term relationship such as marriage.

Teenage sexual relationships

There is a tremendous scatter of normality in teenage sexual behaviour. Some youngsters in remote single-sex schools may show little interest in or have no contact with the opposite sex until eighteen or over, others are in stable sexual relationships by the age of fourteen. Both are within normal limits. By nineteen, 50 per cent of British youngsters, boys and girls, will have experienced sexual intercourse—but only 50 per cent, so either way a nineteen-year-old is 'normal'!

Kinsey reported that up to 30 per cent of young men had some sort of homosexual experiences when growing up. Both boys and girls may be unsure of their sexual orientation for many years—and especially at a single-sex school, where they may become emotionally and physically involved with a same-sex partner. Some such youngsters continue to choose homosexual relationships by preference throughout their lives, whilst others—sometimes those who lacked self-confidence or felt under-developed or unattractive to the opposite sex in their teens—become heterosexual later.

Youngsters often begin their interest in the opposite sex in the safety of a gang. Boys leer at girls and girls giggle at boys—then send ambassadors on their behalf to sound out feelings, before overtly declaring an interest. If their attraction is reciprocated, they may risk being acknowledged as a pair within the gang, then later as a couple. The girls may be more emotionally involved—not always. Both need to prove their attractiveness by having a special relationship, and perhaps need a secret personal life not governed by parental influence. They need someone to love and someone who cares for them. They enjoy the social status of their relationship and the perks that accrue. It serves as a testing-ground to satisfy their sexual curiosity—which may be more important to the boy. They may well become infatuated with each other as these processes coalesce.

But they have a lot to learn and a lot to feel anxious about: with whom do they feel comfortable and relaxed; what should they expect from a relationship; what is fact, what fantasy; how deeply involved should they get and who controls this; how can they learn to trust each other, yet at the same time protect themselves from getting hurt both emotionally and physically? The girl may have more opportunities to share her anxieties with friends and confidantes; boys tend to brag, boast or joke about their conquests, but often cannot confide their secret worries with anyone.

Such has been the lot of youngsters for countless generations. So too have the sexual *myths*:

> That boys know more about sex than girls
> That boys always want sex
> That once aroused, a boy loses control, and so girls
>   must keep control
> That it's cruel to send a boy home with an erection

Both sexes are type-cast by such myths, which pressurise them into a stereotyped behaviour and make them both feel anxious.

At whatever age we *start* sexual interaction with another person, we are bound to feel anxious and unsure and lacking confidence in ourselves. For many youngsters this process is starting sooner than ever—so they must negotiate the private fears about their sexuality at an even more immature stage of personal development and self-confidence.

Girls' fears

Most girls begin with unanswered questions about being touched—will my breasts and genitalia be acceptable to my partner? (Most girls have never seen another's genitalia.) What behaviour will risk pregnancy (who can we ask)? Will what I have been doing show on my face or breasts or genitalia (masturbation, petting, intercourse)? What about VD, herpes, cancer of the cervix? Will having sex with him make him like me more or less? When should I start the pill (see Chapter 4)? When should I live-in with him?

And the most private worries of all—which, like all adolescent tasks, continue throughout our life—are worries about our sexual performance. When inexperienced, a girl may not realise that increased vaginal lubrication is part of sexual arousal. She may feel embarrassed by it—or, once she realises its significance, by the lack of it. She may be aware of the word orgasm, but may never have experienced one, and may be pressurised by her partner into pretending to reach a climax—which, of course, is the most likely way to ensure she will not! Most teenage girls do *not* experience regular climax in lovemaking or petting, for a variety of reasons. They rarely feel totally relaxed in the relationship, which may be transient or uncommitted; they may fear pregnancy; their partner may have little technique (he will not know how to caress her genitalia and she dare not tell him); and the setting for lovemaking may be hurried, furtive and uncomfortable with little opportunity for privacy and relaxation. She may also fear penetration, if she has had little sexual experience, and develop vaginismus or spasms of the lower part of vagina, which prevents consummation of the relationship (see Chapter 3).

Boys' fears

Boys assume they are expected to take the sexual initiative, and must anxiously decide whether or not to 'go further'—a lonely decision, not helped by some girl-friends who demurely and confusingly say 'no' when they really mean 'yes'. He may be unsure what 'further' really means, yet dare not ask. Once he has embarked on full intercourse, a sexually inexperienced young man's fears usually centre around his ability to establish and maintain an erection, and how long he can hold on before he ejaculates. Anxiety is likely to confirm his fears. If his erection has failed in the past (perhaps because of alcohol) he will be even more on edge. Premature ejaculation is normal for young inexperienced men, especially if they have occasional sex only, and this can be extremely embarrassing for them—particularly in a new relationship when they are wanting to impress. Much of the sexual boasting of young men hides the reality of unsatisfactory sexual exploits. For some, these early experiences can put them off relationships for many years, before their personal confidence is sufficient to cope with the threat of sexual failure and the consequent humiliation.

In fact we adults, who envy the youngsters their new-found sexual freedom, would do well to remind ourselves that in theory it may seem great, but in reality, it may well be very different! If teenagers want to share their sexual anxieties with you, be receptive, sympathetic and reassuring. Often listening is all you need to do. They may turn to an alternative adult-figure rather than their own parents, who might be too emotionally caught up to be dispassionate. Don't feel hurt by this—it's normal.

If they want your advice about whether to sleep with someone or not, never give it; simply remind them of the need to take relationships one step at a time, that sexual intercourse usually changes the level of commitment and involvement, and that our personal sex lives are private for good reason. If they are unsure enough to want to share the decision-making, they are probably not ready to take on the responsibility for the privacy and emotional commitment that a sexual relationship usually entails. The Brook Advisory Clinics and many Young People's Contraceptive clinics now exist across Britain; these offer a counselling service as well as contraceptive advice to youngsters grappling with their sexuality—or they can seek advice and free contraception from their family doctor. If they are anxious about pregnancy or venereal disease they should be encouraged to go for medical advice as soon as possible.

3 Adjustment of the Young Couple

As a couple pass from the exhilaration and excitement of their early courtship, and the novelty and enthusiasm to attract and catch a mate is replaced by the social and personal recognition that they have bonded as a pair, so the adjustment period really begins. No longer on their best behaviour with each other, familiarity creeps in and the honeymoon period ends. Those little niggles which seemed so unimportant (or even lovable) before, gradually become a source of preoccupation, irritation or pain—and this may be especially noticeable in the sexual relationship. What was tolerated in a lover, is scorned in a husband or wife. Some couples choose to remain unmarried to avoid this change of label. Others only marry when they have decided to have children—or find themselves pregnant.

The early period of sexual adjustment (whether married or not) is an important time for a couple to sort out some of the 'wrinkles' in their relationship if they are to co-exist comfortably and perhaps form a stable long-term unit in the future. A basic requirement for sorting-out is the ability to *communicate* clearly to each other what are the problems, before they get out of proportion and lead to anger and resentment, which can erode even the most loving relationship. Because good communication is so important I have outlined in detail the basic principles to follow in Chapter 7. If you have difficulty in resolving problems with each other, I do urge you to try them.

Now let us look at some of the areas where good communication can make all the difference to the developing sexual relationship of a young couple.

Sexual ignorance and misunderstandings

Most of us lack confidence in our sexual behaviour, and wonder if we are pleasing our partner or doing it properly! But we fear asking in case we make fools of ourselves, and even more we fear criticising our partner's technique. There is a tremendous taboo on any talk about sex in marriage—yet good sexual communication can transform a physical relationship. You don't need to use words—just put your hand over your partner's and *show* him or her how you like being touched, particularly in more delicate areas such as the genitalia; then ask your partner to *show* you how he or she likes to be touched. Being able to express yourself in this way (and protect yourself if you don't like what's being done to you) really enhances lovemaking. You are *not* dictating to your partner, merely communicating what you like and don't like; it's up to him or her to decide when to do it or not.

Let's look at some of the common misunderstandings about sexual behaviour which can also be cleared up with good communication (and a little factual information, which I hope you will gain from this book).

Who should initiate sex?

Because they think it is 'unfeminine', women often feel reticent about initiating making love—or sulk if their suggestion is turned down; yet it is good if they can share the responsibility with their partner. Each should feel free to say yes or no to sex without fear of reprisal. Reaching an agreement about the frequency of love-making may be quite a problem for some couples with varying sexual appetite. Compromise and goodwill usually succeed in a resolution of the problem, provided the couple are friendly and not harbouring grudges. Remember that sex can be surprisingly enjoyable even when you had thought you weren't in the mood to begin with. But if you are forced into sex against your wishes, it can seem unpleasant and even aggressive, and the consequent resentment produced means that neither partner will enjoy what is happening. It is much better to have a little mutually enjoyable sex than more cold and angry sex.

As a couple accommodate to a regular sexual routine, the frequency of intercourse usually decreases—paradoxically, as the pleasure and satisfaction increases. It is common for couples to report that sex gets better over time. Sexual appetite often increases on holidays, when a couple are more relaxed or in a novel setting, and even at home a little music, soft lights or a drink at bedtime may act as a sexual stimulant from time to time.

Adjustment of the Young Couple

'Foreplay'

In a new relationship, people kiss, caress and fondle each other without thinking before attempting intercourse, and enjoy penetration more as a result of being more highly aroused. But, once sex becomes an established ritual, some couples abandon much kissing and foreplay and concentrate on genital sex. This is unfortunate and usually reduces sexual pleasure. Caressing need not stop when you have intercourse—and it can be an end in itself if you don't feel like intercourse, if you have a period, or if you have just had an operation or a baby. Caressing does not have to lead to intercourse once you are married—it didn't before! Genital caressing is usually necessary if a woman wants to reach orgasm.

Sexual arousal

During sexual arousal several snags may be encountered. A woman may fear she is keeping her partner waiting when he has an erection early in lovemaking, and she may hurry on to vaginal intercourse before she is aroused. An erection does not mean full arousal, and it is much nicer to carry on caressing and kissing until she feels more stimulated. She may also fear that *she* is not aroused because she doesn't have such a clear signal from *her* body. If she is lying on her back, her genitals may feel quite dry even though she is lubricating well—because the secretion remains pooled in her vagina. Some women feel inhibited about becoming sexually aroused because they think it isn't feminine, or makes them seem less attractive.

Both men and women may experience their sexual arousal waxing and waning—for him perhaps with a slight loss of erection. This is normal, but may worry a sexually vulnerable person (and, let's face it, we all are!). The erection usually returns with more stimulation, but may be prevented by anxiety. Problems with erections can beset a man of any age if he is sexually anxious, angry, tired or drunk—or if he has diabetes. If he can get an erection with masturbation or in the early morning, then he can exclude a physical cause for his problem. If he has longstanding problems with his erections then he may need help from a doctor or sexual counsellor. Once a man has experienced a failure of erection, he often develops 'performance anxiety', anticipating failure again and again; and the more he fears, the more likely he is to fail.

My advice to any man or woman with problems of sexual arousal is to set limits for yourself. Don't aim to respond or have intercourse; just set out to enjoy each other's body by touching and kissing, with no goals in mind. Even put a ban on genital touching and just enjoy the physical intimacy of each other's body—showing each other what you like. Call it massage, and try touching each other alternately so you can concentrate wholly on being touched. Indulge yourself and each other! You can get more pleasure and comfort from that than from intercourse if you're not in the mood, or if you're tense or anxious that you won't succeed. Don't forget to show each other what you like. As you become more relaxed and as your confidence returns, so should your responses. For more details of helping sexual problems, see Chapter 8.

Premature ejaculation

'Coming' sooner than you (or your partner) would choose is a common problem among men, but one that neither partner may feel able to talk about with the other. A wife may feel totally disloyal if she mentions it to her doctor or best friend; yet it may ruin lovemaking for her, often causing her to lose interest in sex, or to ask him to get it over with as quickly as possible, so that his problem gets even worse.

In fact, premature ejaculation can easily be helped once the couple admit they have a problem. The sad thing is that many men go through their sexual life not acknowledging it or attempting to learn to delay their orgasm. If you have this problem, see Chapter 7 for details of how to help yourself.

A woman's orgasm

This may be unpredictable in early sexual relationships. Unless she is relaxed, unhurried, trusting her partner and free from anxiety about unwanted pregnancy and from fear of being discovered by her parents or interrupted by young children, she is unlikely to be regularly orgasmic. If she has inhibited attitudes about sex, she may be unresponsive too. But the majority of women and young wives who fail to reach climax do so because neither they nor their partners recognise that they need to be caressed in the area of their clitoris as well as having vaginal intercourse if they wish to reach climax easily. If she can show her partner how she likes to be touched this helps.

It doesn't matter if a couple don't reach climax together—in fact most people prefer to enjoy each other's climax separately (if they have one). But remember that you can have an entirely satisfactory sex life without reaching a climax, so don't pressurise each other to 'go the whole way' every time you touch. For more advice, see Chapter 8.

Vaginismus—non-consummated marriage

Some women 'freeze' whenever they attempt to have full vaginal intercourse. The muscles at the lower end of their vagina go into spasm, and neither the erect penis nor their husband's finger may be allowed through. This condition is called vaginismus and means that the marriage remains unconsummated (and legally can be annulled). Vaginismus is usually caused by fear, although very occasionally there may be a physical problem (such as a thickened hymen) which leads to spasm.

Fear of sexual intercourse is not uncommon, but most women gradually build up confidence in themselves and trust in their partner and learn enough about their own genitalia to realise that if they are relaxed there is plenty of room in their vagina for a penis (and room enough for a baby's head to emerge during childbirth, when the muscles and ligaments are further relaxed by hormonal changes). But some women may have had a painful experience involving their vagina (for example, an insensitive gynaecological examination, an injury during childbirth or a sexual assault), so that any future attempt at penetration raises their anxiety level and vaginal spasm results. With encouragement they can gradually learn to relax, to insert their own finger and then their partner's finger into the vagina, until they feel confident enough to attempt penetration by the penis. Some women prefer to use dilators (with lubrication such as KY Jelly), starting with a small one and progressing to one of equivalent size to their partner's penis.

Another cause of vaginismus appears to be a fear of growing up into mature womanhood. Some women remain closely attached to their parents and although they enjoy keeping house for their husband they do not seem to want a full sexual relationship, which for them implies total separation from their own childhood; nor do they want children of their own. They use their vaginismus as a means of avoiding full womanhood. But it must be emphasised that despite these anxieties, many women with vaginismus do enjoy sexual stimulation, and with petting will reach climax and enjoy lovemaking provided it does not include penetration of the vagina. Therefore, it need not be a problem, provided the partner is happy with his sex life and they do not want to have children. See Chapter 8 for more advice.

Guilt feelings and inhibitions

Some people grow up in an environment where anything remotely connected with sex is taboo. They may have been told off if they asked about the facts of life, and may have experienced a strict and rigid household where sensuality and pleasure was frowned upon. Their parents may never have demonstrated affection either to the child or to each other. At any hint of sex the TV was switched off. The teenage years are particularly fraught for the daughters from such homes, with embargoes on make-up, late nights, boyfriends, pop songs and sexy clothes. They are constantly reminded of the dangers of sex—disgusting, shameful, filthy, dangerous, immoral, painful or infectious. Any form of sensual or physical expression is seen as dirty, self-gratification or sinful, and even undressing is couched in embarrassment and secrecy.

When such people marry, their sex lives are often a misery. To go from such massive prohibitions to seeing sex as pleasant or desirable requires a massive leap in attitudes. If they are lucky enough to marry a patient and uninhibited spouse, their inhibitions may fade as they re-appraise their childhood values and replace them with more appropriate adult ideas—perhaps helped by books such as this, or *The Joy of Sex*, and many magazine articles that give permission to enjoy sex without guilt. Some inhibited men can respond sexually only with a prostitute—keeping their wives pure and unsullied from the filth. Some inhibited women remain sexually uninterested for life, putting up with sex to be a good wife, or in order to have children. Sexual inhibitions may of course also be acquired from sexual assault, or from witnessing domestic violence in childhood, when trust in the opposite sex is destroyed and defences stay high, particularly in vulnerable situations such as physical intimacy.

Problems about self-image

To relax and enjoy sex we need to feel attractive to ourselves as well as to our partner. Anything that damages our self-esteem may damage our sexuality too. For example, unemployment may hit a man or woman above or below the belt! Wives who change from a professional or working role to motherhood and domesticity sometimes feel dull and boring and off sex. Men who enjoyed flirting and 'pulling the birds' as a teenager may feel that in a stable married relationship their wings are clipped, their macho image tarnished and their sexual appetite faded.

Occasionally women dwell morbidly on the shape of their breasts, or on being too fat or too thin, and despite their partner's reassurances, cannot relax and accept themselves as they are. They may wear down their partners by constantly seeking compliments and praise to reduce their self-doubts. It is perhaps a sad reflection that the commercial world has so exploited the 'perfectly packaged body' as the acme of sexual attractiveness, that many people—men and women—are seduced into believing this, and hate themselves as a result. All self-image problems can, of course, be compounded by an insensitive partner who criticises one's shape or size, or compares others more favourably.

Most people start their sex lives lacking confidence, ignorant, anxious, guilty, inhibited an misunderstood—but the exhilaration and excitement of sexual adventures not only carries them through, but leads on to a new phase of sexual pleasure for established and experienced couples who not only know what to expect from sex, but who can contrive to get the best out of it—for the benefit of their relationship and for themselves.

A good physical relationship brings other rewards than short-term sexual pleasure. Often people feel more relaxed, more fulfilled, more self-confident and attractive if that private part of their life is flourishing. They feel needed and part of a social system. A good sex life has positive benefits for the relationship too—enhancing the ties and bonds by mutual dependence, shared secrets, trust and intimacy which all encourage a long-term investment in and commitment to each other. The importance of sex in our life, however, fluctuates as other events impinge on our experience, such as childbirth or an exciting new job. But even if relegated to the background, it still remains a potent force for good or bad, likely to invade our senses and take over our attention in particular circumstances.

If a couple have an unsatisfactory sex life they may adjust to this by relegating sex to a low priority area of life, and continue to co-exist with few problems. Or the sexual problem may impinge powerfully on their minds so that they feel preoccupied, resentful and frustrated much of the time. Whether one or both of the pair react in this way, the discontent is likely to reverberate into their relationship with destructive consequences. Unless they can air their resentment and grievances, and reach some sort of resolution of the problems, their relationship may become very shaky and vulnerable; 70 per cent of the clients attending Marriage Counselling report that sexual difficulties are one of their major problems, although it must be remembered that sexual problems are just as likely to be caused by marital problems as vice versa. For details of self-help, and where to go for help with sexual problems, see Chapter 8 and the list of 'Useful Addresses'.

Having looked at some of the misunderstandings and anxieties that can impede the early stages of a sexual relationship, we should also consider some other problems which inhibit sexual desire or sexual responses.

Problems in the general relationship

When a couple marry and their 'job description' changes from lovers to husband and wife, with this may come new demands and expectations. As the couple have probably come from different home backgrounds and grown up with different views about men's and women's roles in marriage, friction may develop. The male-female power struggle is inevitable in modern relationships as man and woman attempt to be equally assertive, equally important, equally committed to their own personal growth *and* maintaining a good marriage and raising a family. There must be much soul-searching to get it right. This process of accommodation takes time, and can only succeed if the couple communicate their needs and resentments clearly, and resolve difficulties as they arise. Unresolved they may invade our sexual responses and sexual appetite in an unwelcome fashion.

Adjustment of the Young Couple

As you read this, you may think of particular sticking points in your own relationships, which you may recall as triumphs of diplomacy once you resolved them, or as 'running sores' if they remain unsolved. You may also recall the effect they temporarily had on your sex life, both when the differences of opinion became a battle, and when the battle was resolved. It is impossible to review marital problems in a page, but here are some examples to illustrate the point.

Financial responsibility

To begin with, many couples pool their money in a loving fashion, each trusting the other's judgement and sense of fair play in the rosy glow of first love. But soon this may fade to feeling unfairly treated; I have seen many couples with sexual difficulties which were rapidly improved by having separate bank accounts and a negotiated agreement about who was financially responsible and deserving of what! If you feel chronically resentful about money matters, you do not feel loving or sexy towards the person behind it.

Unrealistic expectations from marriage

Some men want their wives to be a combination of flirtatious young lover, capable housekeeper, mother to their children and a mother substitute for themselves—looking after their needs in the way they were accustomed to throughout childhood. Some women want their husbands to be macho, a gentle lover, yet counsellor and father figure who makes them feel as secure and cherished as they felt as a baby. Such conflicting needs are incompatible with an adult, mature and equal relationship. If a dominating man meets a truly passive and dependent woman, they may settle comfortably together at first, but such a lop-sided marriage may well provide an unstable nest to cope with pressures of a growing family.

Some partners treat their spouses as a 'possession', as though marriage implies a total control over the other's behaviour—which inevitably produces problems in time. Others assume that they can carry on their own life totally as before with little commitment to or investment in the relationship—and that rarely works either.

There are no rules of thumb to make such marital adjustments easy for anyone. We all have to work hard at recognising where are the

Coping with Sexual Relationships

idiosyncratic hot spots of our own particular relationship—discussing them in a friendly way with our spouse (perhaps with someone else there to defuse any tension that may arise) and trying to look at alternative strategies that can be tried until we have got it 'right'—both sexually and socially.

Outside involvement

Jealousy and resentment can be felt if a spouse spends too much time with their own family and friends, or on their work or hobbies or on the housework. It's that problem of getting a balance between the individual's needs and the partner's needs—and most couples need time and a few major arguments to find a fair arrangement for each person. If one partner dominates all decision-making, it is easy to see how chronic resentment will gradually undermine the relationship as the more passive member smoulders silently at the inability to imprint his or her own needs and identity on to the pattern of their daily life (see Chapter 7 on communication). It is not uncommon for the silent partner to switch off sexually in protest at the unfair treatment—their ultimate weapon.

Extra-marital sex

It is not unusual for young couples to find themselves faced with this problem. Modern society almost seems to promote infidelity with its emphasis on residential conferences (usually attended by one partner only), weekend workshops, shift duty, evening classes, unemployment and, of course, general 'sexual permissiveness' and the availability of contraception.

To the 'unfaithful' partner an extra-marital experience is often seen as stimulating, exciting and challenging. It boosts self-esteem by reaffirming his or her attractiveness to other people and it may—by its sexual novelty—boost sexual appetite and responses. He or she can, for a night, pretend to be a different person from the old familiar one in the old familiar relationship. At the time it may feel secret, safe, casual and uncommitted. But several factors should have been carefully judged, although when in a state of infatuation or excitement about an extra-marital episode, one is not at one's most rational. It is important to weigh up one's own vulnerability to getting emotionally hooked on the other person by the impact of the experience, and to

40

decide whether that is a risk worth taking. Even more imponderable, one must decide if the third party is even more vulnerable to 'getting hooked', and will therefore be likely to want more contact. The 'unfaithful' one has to weigh up how hidden he or she can keep such behaviour, and must predict what impact it would have if inadvertently revealed to the regular sexual partner. The risks may prove to be more powerful than the pleasures.

Some partners, after a casual lapse in fidelity, become so obsessed with guilt that they feel obliged to 'confess' to relieve their inner tension. This is a short-sighted and selfish solution to the problem—transferring the tension to the innocent partner, who then faces the responsibility for getting an appropriate perspective on the event instead. Most people would naturally feel immediately betrayed and hurt by hearing about a partner's infidelity; but the secondary, long-term effects may be more unpleasant—the feelings of jealousy and mistrust which may long outlive the basic hurt.

An extra-marital affair need not be the kiss of death to a marriage. There are other, more destructive types of marital behaviour such as chronic thoughtlessness and self-centredness, violence or meanness. If kept in proportion, it may be a short sharp trauma in an otherwise happy relationship. Coming to terms with the imperfections of our relationships, rather than idealising them, is an important phase in sexual and personal maturation. Accepting oneself and partner, warts and all, after such an episode can allow the relationship to regain intimacy, security and trust based on a new set of values, which may be more realistic and solid than the original romantic fantasies; but it takes time and tolerance.

Parenthood

A new baby, although a welcome addition in most homes, may also provide the first taste of real differences of opinion between the couple—both in the method of parenting (e.g. should we pick him up when he cries or let him be?) and in the amount of involvement by one or other spouse, causing resentment and jealousy. Unless these grievances are talked about and the air is cleared by a change in behaviour, by compromise and good humour, the resentment can grow and become a vicious circle of bad temper, hurt, withdrawal and polarisation into extreme positions of misunderstanding and misery out of all proportion to the original difference of opinion. Sex does not flourish in such vicious circles.

The presence of children in a family has immense benefit for most couples—a focus for shared pride, interest, involvement, affection; a reason for 'nest-building', holidays and daily routine; a hope for their future and a feeling of immortality, and other bonuses too numerous to list. But some of the benefits may be converted to disadvantages—children's demands on a parent's time, commitment and energy may cause one or other, or both, parents to lose focus on the marital needs, which eventually causes resentment; the buffering effect of the continual presence of children may discourage open discussion of problems between husband and wife which maintains resentment; or one parent may become a 'team' with a child (same sex or opposite sex) to the exclusion of the other partner, which guarantees jealousy and resentment. Maintaining an appropriate balance between the many facets of life and relationships requires a continued sensitivity to 'signals' from our own feelings and from other people's, and regular and repeated scrutiny of these as situations change. Such servicing is essential, not only for the maintenance of a happy family life and the emotional needs of the child, but for the sex life of the parents too.

Children and sex

Although children seem relatively asexual, I would like to touch briefly on their sexual awakening and the effect it has on their parents' own sex lives. Small children may play with their genitals. This is normal and harmless self-exploration or self-stimulation, but if parents have not been comfortable about their own sexuality they may be made anxious by such natural behaviour in their children, and instead of teaching them that such behaviour is acceptable in *private*, they overreact and prohibit the behaviour as disgusting. In the process they may disturb an innocent child so that he or she becomes anxious, guilty and preoccupied and may even begin to masturbate compulsively as a result.

Small children are naturally curious and will want to ask parents about bodies and babies (and even contraception, if prompted by finding an object they don't recognise). They are puzzled by their parents' bizarre reactions to such ordinary questions; even simple sex education is difficult if parents have not accepted sexuality and reproduction as a normal course of events. There are excellent simple books on sex education for children such as *How a Baby is Made* (Piccolo), which teach not only the children, but also their parents how to approach the subject, and perhaps allow the parents to become sexually more accepting and less inhibited too.

Even in childhood the interchange between a child and parent provides a powerful learning experience for the child's future sexual development. The child will be learning from Mum or Dad what feminine or masculine means (in their household); what marriage is all about; and what tactics work and don't work when trying to manipulate the emotions of an archetypal man (Dad) and woman (Mum). Tragically a few youngsters learn in childhood to mistrust close relationships with men or women, because their early dependency and trust has been rewarded with physical violence, totally unpredictable parental behaviour or the sudden loss of a loved one. Some suffer the trauma of an incestuous experience with a family member—that gross sexual violation of the vulnerability, trust and dependency of a child on adult authority which not only destroys a basic moral code, but may upset the child's ability to enjoy intimacy in the future.

Parents often worry about the children's attitude to their adult sexuality. Should they show physical affection for each other in front of the children, or will they feel jealous and left out? The answer is 'go ahead'—provided you stick to the same socially conventional limits that you would adopt in the presence of any other adult. A child feels emotionally secure, protected and reassured about the stability of his parental relationship by seeing signs of their affection. He is also learning important lessons about expressing affection, so carry on—of course remembering to include the children (within limits) in your physical demonstrations too. Incidentally, boys need cuddling as much as girls; it makes them emotionally tougher, not soft as sometimes believed.

In small houses children inadvertently interfere with their parents' sex life in a variety of ways. A small baby in the parents' bedroom can have a remarkable impact on sexual responses—one whimper and they are gone! Or, because of the fear of waking up a problem sleeper, the responses may never begin. A toddler may toddle in mid-way (a lock on the door can surely be arranged for such eventualities—or the child can be taught to knock or call). The fear of being heard when making love is another anxiety for young parents in small modern houses. This fear may be enough to inhibit orgasm in either sex. Try a bedside radio, or a different time of night or day when interruptions are less; or perhaps accept that, provided children are not frightened or alarmed by what they hear, the knowledge of the parents making *love* should be reassuring. Allowing children to witness sexual behaviour, however, violates both their privacy and ours and is totally inappropriate.

Fathers and daughters may find early adolescence a tricky time for their relationship. He will have to decide (perhaps before her) that having his daughter sit on his knee, or tickling her, is no longer appropriate as she is 'now too old for that sort of thing'. A sensitive Dad can do this with humour and gentleness, avoiding letting his daughter feel rejected. He needs also to learn how to compliment her when she lacks self-confidence; praise from him may mean more than he realises at this sensitive age. Similar issues occur between mother and sons too. A sensitive distinction is needed (yet again) between reassuring an insecure nubile youngster and flirting inappropriately with him or her. There is more about parents and teenagers in Chapter 5.

4 Sex, Reproduction and Illness

The first part of this chapter must be biased towards the female, because a woman's physiology and her emotions are so intimately caught up with her menstrual cycle and reproduction; but make no mistake, most men are intimately caught up with their partner's physiology and emotions too, so the men shouldn't skip this chapter either.

Let's start with a couple's adjustment to the woman's monthly cycle.

Menstruation

Most women under 50 menstruate roughly once a month unless pregnant. So each couple has to decide how to incorporate this monthly event into their sexual relationship over a significant portion of their lifetime. Many ancient cultures had powerful taboos and myths about menstruating women, and even today many couples assume that for the duration of a woman's menstrual flow they should avoid sexual intercourse. For some this will be because of a temporary inhibition of sexual drive, for others because of the practical difficulties of coping with sex and menstruation, and for a few women because they feel discomfort with their period (dysmenorrhoea) or feel sexually unattractive.

But many couples continue with limited love-making during a period—caressing each other to climax without intercourse which, of course, is made much more possible if a woman uses a tampon to cope with her period. Other women keep a contraceptive Dutch cap for use during a period to allow the freedom of normal sexual intercourse without fear of staining. Many just carry on their sex lives normally, accepting that blood is no messier than ejaculate. Each couple must decide for themselves what seems appropriate, which may depend on their sexual appetite. Some women report an increase in sexual interest during menstruation, which may be due to hormonal variations. There is in any case an enormous variation in women's level of sexual interest—for some, it is raised mid-cycle, for others before or after the period. A woman's vaginal secretions change as her hormone levels alter through the month (this fact is used to determine the safe period in the Billings method of natural conception) and this may influence how she interprets her sexual interest and arousal.

Premenstrual tension (PMT)

This is a common problem, particularly in a woman's teens and again in her thirties and forties. Many women in the week before a period feel irritable, bloated and physically and psychologically tense with headache, abdominal discomfort and breast tenderness, usually associated with fluid retention and slight weight gain. Sexual interest may be decreased or absent or sexual relationship may be temporarily disrupted by unpredictable mood swings or depression.

Premenstrual tension may be helped by the contraceptive pill, by a low salt and low fluid diet, by vitamin B_6, or by progesterone tablets—prescribed by the family doctor. Some women taking the contraceptive pill are less prone to PMT; others continue to experience it whilst on the pill. Relaxation or yoga exercises can be helpful and it is useful to keep a diary to avoid, where possible, onerous tasks in the premenstrual phase of the month.

Sex and contraception

The oral contraceptive or pill

One of the commonest contraceptives, especially for under 35-year-olds, the pill works by preventing ovulation and/or implantation of the embryo and is the most effective method of contraception. A small proportion of women (up to 10 per cent) report a decrease in sexual desire when on the pill, sometimes with depression, and in some cases this may cause a women to reject this method. Scientists' views conflict over whether this loss of sexual interest is caused by hormonal changes, by the loss of possibility of pregnancy, by the fear of side-effects from the pill, or by resentment at having to take sole responsibility for contraception; it is probably a different combination of factors in different women. Vaginal secretion may lessen slightly with the use of the pill, and this may also affect a woman's experience of sexual desire. A few women have irregular or prolonged bleeding with the pill, which upsets their sex life, but the majority remain happily and successfully on the contraceptive pill with no change in their sexual relationships except for the better because they have lost the fear of pregnancy.

The morning-after pill, which must be taken within seventy-two hours of unprotected intercourse, is now available in an emergency for women who fear an unwanted pregnancy—but this is not suitable as a regular form of contraception, and should be used in crisis only.

The free availability of the contraceptive pill for unmarried youngsters over the age of sixteen now presents the teenage generation with a new set of problems about their sexual behaviour. Taking the pill implies not only admission of an active sexual life, but that it is premeditated and planned rather than 'taken by surprise'. Their responsible choice to use contraception may be misinterpreted by angry parents as an open invitation to casual sex, whereas an unwanted pregnancy may be seen as a more acceptable 'mistake' in that it was less planned in cold blood (a rather short-term view but sadly one that still persists). When a girl ends her relationship with a particular boy-friend, she has to decide whether or not to continue taking the pill, and at what stage in any subsequent relationships to tell her new partner she is so protected.

The intrauterine contraceptive device (IUCD) or coil

This is a popular method of contraception for women who have already experienced childbirth or an abortion, because then it is less likely to be rejected by their uterus, and is unlikely to cause infection. Inserted by a family doctor or family planning clinic, it stays in the uterus for several years and probably works by preventing implantation of the fertilised egg. A few women experience heavier periods or abdominal cramps but for most, the IUCD remains in place with no side-effects. It is an effective form of contraception, and causes virtually no upset to a woman's sexuality or to her responses unless it prolongs her periods, or interferes with her need to experience the possibility of pregnancy for sexual pleasure.

The cervical cap or Dutch cap

A mechanical barrier to contraception, this must be inserted into the vagina to cover the cervix before intercourse, having first been coated with a spermicidal cream. Its contraceptive efficiency lasts for about three hours and it must remain in position for at least six hours after intercourse. Although its mechanical presence should not interfere with the physical pleasure of intercourse for either the man or woman (if it is inserted correctly), the hassle of inserting the cap and the

unpredictableness of whether it will be made use of (if you *don't* put it
in, he *will* feel like sex, if you *do*—he's snoring when you get to bed)
may lead to resentments. The need to be consistent and scrupulously
careful to insert the cap regularly before intercourse makes it a
difficult form of contraception for an unmarried youngster to organise,
although older women may prefer it, feeling in control of making
decisions about contraception from day to day.

Some women tend to brandish their intention to insert their cap as a
sexual challenge or test for their partner—a test he may fail because
he resents being so coerced, or because his anxiety about the proposed
performance causes problems with getting an erection (many, of
course, rise to the challenge with pleasure!).

The sheath

This used to be the main method of contraception; it relies upon the
forward planning and responsibility of the *man* in most cases. The
condom or sheath is still a popular form of contraception for many
people, young and old. It has certain advantages—it is relatively
reliable (if used with *each* act of intercourse) and for some men it
reduces the likelihood of premature ejaculation because the intensity of
stimulation is usually decreased. Some women appreciate the reduction
in mess with ejaculation, and the risk of venereal disease is reduced
too.

The use of a sheath in a sexually experienced couple can be
incorporated into their lovemaking without interruption in continuity or
'atmosphere', but in a sexually unsure young man the same procedure
may produce great loss of dignity, embarrassment, and sometimes loss
of erection. Even going into a chemist's to purchase a sheath may be
an impossible hurdle—and of course the cost may be another barrier to
be negotiated. Couples may share contraceptive responsibility between
cap and sheath, relying on the safe period in between.

Safe period or rhythm method

Some people, for religious reasons or because they cannot tolerate
other contraceptive methods, prefer to rely on regulating their fertility
by natural means. They try to predict when the woman is most
fertile—that is, at the time of ovulation—and avoid intercourse for

three days both before and after this time. The problem is that, unless a woman's periods are totally predictable like clockwork, the time of ovulation may vary from month to month. It usually occurs two weeks *before* the next period (which means that it can only be pinpointed with accuracy in retrospect). A woman's temperature may go up slightly when ovulation occurs, and her vaginal secretion alters in character. To ensure that the rhythm method of contraception is reliable, a woman should be taught to understand her secretions, keep regular charts, and discuss the method with a trained counsellor. Even then, it is less reliable than all other methods of contraception, and interrupts her sex life more than all other methods.

Withdrawal or coitus interruptus

Although this method is practised by many couples, the attempt both to enjoy the pleasures of sex in a relaxed, comfortable and sexually aroused fashion, and at the same time to be on guard to withdraw the penis from the vagina before reaching the 'point of no return'—and ejaculation—usually leads to sexual tension. If a couple rely on this method of contraception regularly, it may reduce their sexual desire and their sexual pleasure and may inhibit her arousal or orgasm. It is not reliable, because sperm are sometimes present in the beads of lubrication which may exude from the penis before ejaculation.

Sterilisation

Both male and female sterilisation can now be performed easily and safely. Although the procedure is slightly more complex and risky in the female (usually requiring a general anaesthetic), it continues to be more commonly the woman who agrees to her fallopian tubes being tied rather than her husband's vas deferens. This may be partly because women find it easier to go to the doctor, are more used to gynaecological procedures and are more affected by an extra unwanted pregnancy than a man. Both she and he may fear what effects male sterilisation may have on his potency and masculinity, and his alarm may be sufficient to persuade her that life will be easier if *she* shoulders the responsibility. Theoretically, sterilisation does not change our physiology or our capacity to respond sexually, but it may affect how we view ourselves and a minority of men and women take some time to re-establish their sense of masculinity or femininity after sterilisation, during which their sexual desire may temporarily decline. (Hysterectomy may produce a similar temporary effect.)

Infertility

If a couple suspect they may be infertile, or become over-anxious about conception, this may interfere with their sexual desire or function. A couple may be advised to restrict their sexual activity to certain advantageous dates in the month, but find that they suffer a paradoxical inhibition of sexual appetite at this time or fail to become aroused as normal due to the intense pressure to perform by the calendar rather than spontaneously. If infertility is confirmed in one of the pair, all sorts of new issues will appear—guilt, resentment, shame, pity, confusion of loyalties. Many couples come through such a revelation feeling closer and more committed to each other; a few drift apart. Their sexual relationship will often change in response to the declared infertility, and often for the better; the pressure to conceive or avoid conception is now over, and they can get on with the business of co-existing instead!

Now we should look at the opposite but fortunately more common reproductive event.

Pregnancy and sexual relationships

In early pregnancy a woman may feel less interested in sex than later on. She may feel nauseated, irritable and bloated, yet show few outward signs of pregnancy. Her breasts are often sore and engorged and even painful to touch, making her even less keen on caressing and cuddling. She may also fear that lovemaking will bring on a miscarriage (not without foundation, if she has previously miscarried before three months of pregnancy), and may avoid sex as a result. Her partner may fear harming the foetus even more, and their joint preoccupation with the excitement of the pregnancy (especially if it is their first child) can override their sexual appetite.

In the middle three months of pregnancy some women not only return to their normal sexual drive, but may experience a heightened sexual appetite and enjoyment and some become orgasmic for the first time in their lives. It is a relatively safe time for sexual intercourse, and both partners may revel in the freedom from the need for contracpeption. However, if a woman continues to feel unwell, or if the couple remain unduly anxious about the baby, then lovemaking may continue to be inhibited.

As the baby grows larger, and its physical presence impedes conventional positions for intercourse, couples must decide whether to experiment with new approaches to lovemaking (side by side or approaching her vagina from behind or with her on top), whether to abandon intercourse in favour of mutual caressing—or whether to wind down their sexual activity until after childbirth. As a woman nears term her uterus becomes more sensitive and she may feel uncomfortable contractions during orgasm.

A new baby and the sexual relationship

A considerable number of women lose interest in sex after the birth of a baby for up to six months or even longer. Although this may be related to post-natal depression it often is not, and we should look for other explanations. First, she will be tired and physically not at her best. Her hormones may not be back to their normal balance, making her irritable and moody if not depressed. Her vagina may still feel sore or stitched or stretched, and she may continue to have a discharge for some weeks after her baby is born. Her breasts may be engorged with milk or sore and feel sexually unattractive to her—added to which her stomach may not yet have resumed its normal shape, and the stretch marks may still seem prominent and ugly, affecting her view of herself and her sexiness. Emotionally she will be putting much of her energy into the challenge of motherhood; the demands of her new-born baby foster her maternal instinct of love, and anxiety—both powerful feelings which may temporarily eclipse the emotions towards her husband. In fact any demand *he* makes on her may seem like an unnecessary intrusion on this new and precious relationship. His physical presence may seem gross and hairy in comparison with the baby's softness and sweetness. She may even temporarily be sated with the pleasures of the physical intimacy of cuddling and suckling her baby and need no other form of physical contact. And there is the 'role-confusion' of trying to be both maternal and sexual in our society—roles which tend to contradict each other.

But we must look at his problems too. Suddenly he is in second place—feeling ignored and out in the cold with a rival (especially marked if the baby is a son) taking his wife's attentions. Unlike her, his body has *not* undergone a series of hormonal and physical changes and his sexual appetite may be intact and frustrated after several weeks abstinence. He may not see any role for himself with the baby, especially if she is breast feeding. He may feel hurt if his wife seems continually irritable and critical, and if he tries to turn to sex for reassurance he may feel further rejected.

Fortunately most of these early problems resolve themselves, but both partners should make every endeavour, at this critical readjustment stage of early parenthood, to find an acceptable balance between their parenting roles and their marital roles. It is particularly important to be on guard for well-meaning but inappropriate interference to this adjustment by parents or parents-in-law, who tend to side with their offspring against the spouse. It is important to re-establish a happy sexual relationship with each other after childbirth, and this may again take time, goodwill and good communication to get it right! A period of limited love-making short of intercourse may help (see Chapter 8).

The menopause

When a woman faces the cessation of her monthly periods, she may become acutely aware of the aging process, as the decreasing oestrogen and progesterone levels alter the subcutaneous fat content and moisture content of her all-important skin. She may have to endure a phase of hot flushes and hot sweats too, perhaps with heavy, irregular or unpredictable periods for a time and an increase in weight. The lining of her vagina will produce less lubrication. All these things do not help her feelings of sexual attractiveness! Once her periods have stopped and the physical changes are over, she then has to adjust to the psychological reality of being infertile for the rest of her sexual life. For some women, this is a great relief—their contraceptive era is past—while for others it is a time of regret or nostalgia, especially if they would have liked more children or if they were infertile before the menopause. To some people the possibility of pregnancy seems to be a necessary ingredient for sexual enjoyment and without it (for example, when already pregnant, when taking the contraceptive pill or after the menopause) sexual interest and pleasure fades.

One thing is quite certain—a woman after the menopause is still capable of responding sexually and having orgasms, because her body continues to produce enough oestrogen in her fifties and sixties to maintain her sexual function. *But*—and this is important—if she does not maintain regular sexual activity (at least once a fortnight) then the lining of her vagina will become thinner and less well lubricated, and the passage may contract so that intercourse can become painful or impossible. Many post-menopausal women need to add a lubricant during lovemaking (such as KY Jelly) as their natural secretion will be less than before. KY jelly is a useful aid to lovemaking at any age— any chemist will stock it.

Hysterectomy

Some women need to have a hysterectomy operation (the removal of the womb and cervix) with or without removal of the ovaries. If the ovaries are removed, they will experience the symptoms of the menopause. A hysterectomy operation should not—and usually does not—upset the sexual relationship of a couple; in fact it often improves it, as the gynaecological condition that necessitated it is removed. After hysterectomy a woman can still lubricate and respond as before and experience climax, although it may feel different. Some women, however, do find that they lose interest in sex.

Prostate problems

Men in later years may have trouble with their prostate gland—a hidden gland at the neck of the bladder which, if enlarged, causes increasing difficulty in passing water. If this becomes a major problem, then it may cause back pressure on the kidneys or retention of urine, and a prostate operation (prostatectomy) may be necessary. This is a common operation and although, in many cases, it causes no sexual difficulties thereafter, in a few cases men can develop 'retrograde ejaculation', which means that, although they have a normal erection and reach a climax in the normal way, when they ejaculate their semen passes into the bladder instead of out through the penis. There is little that can be done to prevent this from happening, and most couples quickly adapt to the new state of affairs—in fact, some wives rejoice in the lack of mopping up after lovemaking!

Mastectomy

After mastectomy, many couples experience great difficulty in returning to a normal sex life. The loss of a breast can have a powerful impact on a woman's sense of attractiveness and self-esteem, and it is helpful if the couple can rehearse some of these problems with each other and a counsellor *before* the breast is removed, and if they can start physical contact and caressing as soon as possible after the operation. I advise women after a mastectomy to leave their bra on and to aim for *limited* touching to begin with—not aiming for intercourse or orgasm. This applies after *any* operation or illness; provided a couple have agreed with each other to set limits, simple touching and petting or caressing can be most reassuring, relaxing, or even stimulating, and can do much to restore the intimacy and familiarity with each other after the strain of a period of hospitalisation or illness, whether or not there has been an operation.

Coronary heart disease

After a coronary many men and their partners feel most anxious about resuming lovemaking; 'Will it cause another coronary?' is the commonest anxiety. Most physicians advise that if you can climb two flights of stairs without getting angina (pain in the chest) then you can cope with conventional lovemaking—but it has been shown to be more dangerous to indulge in the heightened stimulation of extra-marital sex! Some men develop difficulties in getting or keeping an erection after a coronary. This is *not* a physical effect of the heart disease, but a psychological effect that they no longer feel potent; the coronary has shattered their self-confidence in the same way that redundancy might do. Such problems can be overcome by patience, reassurance and the gradual regaining of self-esteem.

Diabetes and strokes may also upset sexual function, and so may certain medicines—especially those for high blood pressure—so if you are taking tablets and have trouble with your erections or sexual responses, ask your doctor to try a different drug for you.

Physical disability

Physical disability may be so severe that it prevents the regular socialising that is usually necessary to meet a sexual partner. Social clubs for disabled teenagers and adults are rare, because of the difficulties in transport and dependence on others for mobility. It is sad that such a low priority is given to the social and personal needs of disabled people. Similarly, any suggestion that a severely disabled person might wish to masturbate or to have casual sexual relations is seen as unnatural or indecent.

Physical difficulties afflict a significant proportion of the population, but rarely receive public interest or concern. But if you stop to consider that there is no difference in sexual development because people are blind or deaf or spastic, you will quickly envisage their special problems. Far too little attention is usually paid to their sex education and sexual development.

Many of us acquire physical disabilities later in life, such as arthritis, or paralysis after a head injury or stroke, and our sex life has to readjust accordingly. The victim may need to reappraise his or her body image and sense of attractiveness, as well as having to reorganise suitable positions for sexual intercourse, or altering the form of sexual behaviour to accommodate for particular problems such as fixed hips, or permanent problems with erections. For the spouse there may be the added problem of trying to be both nurse and lover, and the anxiety and perhaps distaste about the physical and sometimes personality changes that have occurred in a recently disabled partner. Visiting contraceptive services are available for housebound people, but they are rarely used—presumably because of the embarrassment of acknowledging their sexuality.

Mental handicap

Parents with mentally handicapped youngsters face particular problems during the sexual development of their offspring. It is usual nowadays to attempt to maintain mildly to moderately handicapped people in the community rather than in institutions. Parents, teachers and staff at adult training centres need to pay particular attention to repeating information time and time again until the youngster understands about menstrual hygiene and the facts of life, about the need for privacy with masturbation, about the need to avoid being sexually exploited or hurt, especially if the mentally handicapped youngster is an attractive girl. Some parents are so anxious about their handicapped child's sexuality that they keep them rigidly away from the opposite sex, thus depriving them of an important facet of their life—special relationships of their own. Many mentally handicapped youngsters simply want to hold hands or kiss and cuddle, to feel they have a special relationship. Their interest in sexual intercourse is often low, but if they do form a regular close relationship then they should be protected from pregnancy. Fear of pregnancy is only one problem. Parents often fear social disapproval if their mentally handicapped youngster is allowed to mix with the opposite sex, or fear that they will be sexually irresponsible; yet they are no more likely to cause sexual offence than adolescents of normal intelligence—probably less. If they marry they are less fertile, with 15 per cent chance that their offspring will be handicapped too (if one parent is handicapped). Mentally handicapped people are often loyal, loving and trustworthy and I have known them make happy and caring partners and good parents.

5 Mature Relationships

It is a myth that once married, we live happily ever after—we don't! Throughout adult life we continue to pass through transitions, and each stage presents us, and our close relationships, with new challenges. We have already looked at some of these—adjusting to marriage and adjusting to parenthood. Although these are *shared* experiences in a marriage they may affect the husband and wife very differently. Other transitional stages may be unique to one of the pair—such as starting a new career, facing an operation, or losing a parent; but you can be sure that the effects of such unilateral experience will nevertheless reverberate through the marriage. There is no such thing as an uninvolved partner! They will also reverberate through the couple's sex life. It is unusual to be able to divorce our sexual interest and responses from the happenings in our personal lives and marriage— although a few hardy couples appear to continue enjoying sex through the most ghastly crises.

Many couples look back on their middle years—perhaps with children at school—as their happiest and most fulfilled. Life is often more stable and predictable, and the couple have probably sorted through the early adjustment in their physical and general relationships. Some women may only begin experiencing consistent orgasms in their thirties and forties, at last feeling sexually confident, less inhibited and socially more secure. Ironically, most men reach their peak of sexual interest and responsiveness in their late teens and early twenties; then their latent period (the time necessary before they can achieve another erection) gradually increases from the thirties onwards. Most women, on the other hand, reach their peak of sexual interest in their late thirties, when their partners may be sexually on the wane.

Problems with self-image

But general rules cannot be made about sex and marriage. A woman may be experiencing the 'depressed housewife' syndrome in her early thirties—with a husband frequently absent or over-involved with work, a poor relationship when he *is* at home, children out at school or toddlers under her feet all day, no job to call her own except

housework, few opportunities for personal social contacts, and little
money to alleviate the misery. She may eat for solace, gaining weight
as a result, and feel increasingly dejected and unattractive. Not
surprisingly, she often complains that in bed she feels 'dead from the
neck down'.

How can she help her sexual problem? Well, the answer is to try to
improve how she feels about herself. If we do not feel reasonably good
about ourselves we are unlikely to feel good about our sexuality, or
want to share it with someone else. Boosting our self-esteem takes
quite an effort if we are feeling depressed. We should be as tolerant,
reassuring and cosseting of ourselves as we are naturally with other
people—I call it being your own parent. We should also encourage
ourselves to go for a walk, write letters, meet people, visit friends,
wash our hair, buy new clothes, take up a new interest, lose weight,
exercise or whatever we would advise someone *else* to do.

Social contacts are important for most, although not all people.
Apart from someone to tell our troubles to, friends impart a sense of
belonging and security which makes us feel more accepted, more
attractive and often more sexy. I have known women who had
completely lost interest in sex until they started a part-time job or
joined a women's organisation or group--weight watchers or mother
and toddlers' club—or started taking in bed and breakfast guests.

Men facing redundancy or unemployment may find sexual problems
developing for the first time in their lives too, for similar reasons to
the depressed housewife. Many of them will be in traditional
relationships with set views of the man's role and the woman's role in
marriage—he to work, bring home the money and be boss, and she to
run the home as his unpaid housekeeper. If he loses his job, their
whole existence is changed. His loss of role, loss of finance and loss of
occupation may seriously affect his self-esteem and self-confidence. He
may try to fill up time helping in the house, which undermines his
wife's role and invades her territory. Ironically a wife, who may or
may not have worked throughout her marriage, often has less of a
problem adjusting to her own unemployment because her life has
always been shared between work, the home and relationships in a
more stable distribution than her husband's over-emphasis on his
work. The depression and marital strain of unemployment tells not
only on the couple and their sexual relationship (it is a common time
for problems with erections to develop), but also on their youngsters as

family tensions rise. The tragedy of the current unemployment figures is that such misery goes unrecognised, because it does not increase hospital admissions or produce serious illness.

A depressed housewife or unemployed husband is often made worse by her or his spouse. It may be necessary for the spouse to be persuaded to change behaviour and attitudes too—such as making an effort to reduce working hours (even if he or she is a 'workaholic') and being more involved in the family, more receptive to listening to the domestic daily round, and accepting that the problems and difficulties (with the shopkeeper, children or Hoover) are as irritating as the problems with the foreman, nursing officer or secretary may be. If two people show sensitivity and respect for each other's experiences and feelings, they are both more likely to avoid depression and enjoy each other's company, working or not. Each should ensure that there is time and space made to hear about each other's day and aim to *praise* rather than criticise the other's behaviour. A depressed woman can be enormously encouraged by discovering that her compliments to her husband are as important as his are to her.

Physical changes

Throughout life our self-esteem remains governed not only by our self-image but also by our body image, and middle age is no exception. From thirty-five onward, we become increasingly aware of the physical aging process. It affects our fitness, our body shape and possibly our weight. Wrinkles begin to appear and the skin texture gradually changes. Both sexes may become preoccupied with their sagging bodies—camouflaging them with clothes, make-up, hair-styles, dieting and exercise. In order to maintain a continuing acceptance of our sexual attractiveness and right to sexual expression in middle life it is important to shift the focus of our sex-appeal from how we look to how we are. The way we perceive our partner must be similarly readjusted if we are to continue to find him or her attractive to us. Mercifully, as we progress through life's experiences, most people's character does become deeper, more confident, more interesting and more attractive as their looks fade.

Sexual inhibitions may become noticeably less as the process of maturing occurs and there is less emphasis on the 'body beautiful'. I have known many women who only started leaving their nightdress off in mid-life—long after their physical peak— and men who at last stopped worrying about their baldness or small genitalia or guilt feelings, and started to enjoy their sex life late. But at the same time a middle-aged man may find, for the first time ever, that his erections are not so reliable—particularly if he's tired or has drunk a moderate amount of alcohol. This need not be a problem if the couple don't panic but accept the changes as a normal part of aging; he can usually get his erection back with patience. But if he and his wife become alarmed they develop so-called 'performance anxiety', and become spectators to his sexual responses instead of enjoying their physical intimacy. Each may be checking his penis for hardness—preoccupied with performance instead of pleasure. Remember, a lot of good sexual experiences can be had without a full erection. See Chapter 8 for self-help with sexual problems.

Many of the traditional hurdles of later middle-age and beyond are not readily identifiable. We begin to feel tired more quickly, and perhaps have less zest for anything too energetic or stimulating—keeping warm may take precedence over making love!—or we may have to weigh up the physical discomfort of manoeuvring a bad back or rheumatic hip joints into position, against the pleasure of sexual arousal; and after a long marriage, sex may seem too predictable or even boring to make the necessary effort. Our partner may no longer physically attract us, or even downright repel us, despite our general commitment to stay together. Perhaps secret fantasies and eyes closed during love-making may help—or bedside music, a late night drink, an alternative setting, a newly decorated bedroom, or attractive night-wear; it's amazing what 'seasoning' can do to our taste buds!

The fact that men do *not* have to cope with the powerful psychological hurdle of the menopause allows their aging to be a more gradual and less heart-searching experience. Their self-esteem and sexual attractiveness is rarely so wrapped up with their physical appearance and youthfulness as a woman's tends to be. They have fewer problems in continuing to feel attractive, especially if they are successful, powerful or financially secure (these same attributes in a *woman* can have the opposite effect in making her feel threatening to a man rather than attractive).

Arguments

The sex life of a mature couple continues to be as vulnerable to the vagaries of their general relationship as that of a younger couple.

Differences of opinion exist in most relationships; so does the male/female power struggle. Deciding which partner's needs take priority is a long-term battle for many relationships. Some give up the struggle and acquiesce to the 'stronger' person—but not without cost. Unspoken resentment is probably the commonest cause of sexual problems in middle-aged couples. Although disturbing the marital peace by voicing such resentments seems in the short term to 'rock the boat', in the long term it is likely to lead to a healthier relationship if problems can be thoroughly and bilaterally aired, then resolved or accepted. Some couples who have been together for a long time tend to take up established or entrenched positions about regular domestic disputes—failing either to listen to their partner effectively or sympathetically, or to explain their own view without becoming overheated or aggressive in the process. Children may get drawn into arguments as reinforcements for one or other side too. Partners tend to guess what their spouse will think about something before they have asked, and become angry, defensive or contemptuous in anticipation of this predicted response—'I don't suppose you'll want to go to the pictures'. Resentments do not get aired but smoulder on, with the resultant angry smoke screen effectively blotting out natural sexual interest and responses. In the course of many years counselling sexual problems I have found myself listening to angry feelings, and then arbitrating negotiated settlements about money, in-laws, holidays, hobbies, domestic chores, car maintenance and gardening—to name just a few; yet all were highly relevant to the cause of a particular couple's sexual difficulty, be it problems with erection, orgasm or sexual appetite. The same principles of good communication apply as much to older couples as to any other; see Chapter 8 if you have problems.

Parents, teenagers and sex

One particular area of concern for many middle-aged couples, which can have direct or indirect implications for their sexual adjustment, is their changing relationship with teenage children. As a youngster's need to self-regulate overtakes his desire to be protected by his parents, he swings from feeling totally self-confident one minute to needing control and advice the next. The wise parent can gradually lengthen the 'apron-string' until the youngster can cope alone—but it is a stormy time, especially if the parents cannot agree about what is appropriate, or if one parent is reluctant to give up the parenting role. (Similar storms may be experienced when elderly parents reach the reverse stage of *becoming* dependent on their adult son or daughter—their resentment and ambivalence sends shock-waves through the marriage too.)

In the area of a youngster's developing sexuality the storms are particularly heavy. There are the 'double standards' to be negotiated. What is acceptable to parents as jokes, newspapers, pictures or TV situation comedies is not necessarily acceptable if one's own youngsters do the same thing. Dad may foam at the mouth over a luscious blonde on the street, but forbid his daughter from going out in the same low-cut tee-shirt. He may have one rule for sons and another for daughters—sex is all right for him but *not* for her. Eldest, youngest and only children may experience greater trouble in leaving the nest than middle children. Eldest or only children have the onerous task of educating their parents about current adolescent behaviour to replace their outdated views: 'When I was a lad we never dreamt of . . .'.

Part of parental objections to teenagers' life-style may well be seen as 'sour grapes'. Despite unemployment, most youngsters *do* have many more opportunities than their parents had for travel, further education, financial support, self-expression and self-assertiveness, access to contraception and the opportunities to flout sexual convention. The heavy proscriptions of religion, social conventions, national service and so forth are things of the past, but may have influenced Mum and Dad. Parents also tend to use their own childhood experiences as a model for what was right—and they are mystified by today's teenage behaviour which bears no resemblance to their lives, and leaves their authority in confusion. Teenage sexual behaviour has indeed changed dramatically in the last 20 years, as has drinking behaviour, smoking and the use of drugs.

Other, more subtle objections to teenage sexual development may crop up within a family. A flirtatious nubile daughter can become a threat to an aging wife—both to her own self-image and to her relationship with her husband, whose eyes are no longer on her. Her daughter's flowering sexuality may remind her not only that hers is fading, but that her maternal role is fading too. Dad can have similar feelings about his burly teenage son.

Whilst parents are putting heavy pressure on their teenage

youngsters to be careful of the dangers of sex—fully aware of the risks of pregnancy, venereal disease, emotional and physical hurt or exploitation—they may inadvertently put themselves off sex too. It is a pity that more parents do not use this time of developing sexual awareness and curiosity in their youngsters to offer a friendly ear, information, reassurance and advice, sharing the anxiety and uncertainties about their developing relationships rather than criticising, being dogmatic or ignoring them. Sensible parents can use the time when their youngsters are grappling with their own sexual identity to re-question, readjust and consolidate their own sexual attitudes, values and behaviour too.

Parents often have problems accepting their offspring's choice of boyfriend or girlfriend, especially during those early experimental stages. The more violently the parents react, the more their youngsters will dig in their heels. Parental disapproval seems to fire the need to rebel, and may add fuel to the youngsters' infatuation. Many a teenage marriage has been the result of such opposition, when a little more discretion and tolerance from the adults might have avoided this. Teenage marriages have a high casualty rate for many reasons. They are often precipitated by an unexpected pregnancy, by tensions in the family background, or by a romantic mix of unrealistic expectations, sexual infatuation and blissful ignorance. None of these makes a good formula for the long term. Parental reactions are even more pronounced if their youngsters experiment with homosexual relationships, often amounting to total rejection of the youngsters at a time when they are at their most confused and anxious and most in need of support (see Chapter 6).

Empty nest

The 'empty nest' syndrome may occur when the last teenager has left and suddenly the child-buffering of the last twenty years or more is gone, leaving husband and wife painfully close and undistracted in a way that seems unfamiliar and unrehearsed (she may well have been pregnant when they married and they may have had *no* experience of life together as a couple). Even if they had a spell together before the children, they were different people then anyway. Many marriages cannot cope with the strain of readjusting to this change, which requires flexibility, adaptability and basic goodwill. If a couple barely communicate with each other or cannot express dissatisfaction and anger except in destructive fashion, they do not adapt; they co-exist in a cold war situation, each going their separate ways, often with a total breakdown of the physical relationship too. Not surprisingly, this is a common time for extra-marital relationships and divorce. But the couples who are able to readjust to their new-found freedom often report that these middle years are good and rewarding. They are personally self-confident and mature, they have ironed out most of the wrinkles in their relationship and they can still enjoy sex with each other untroubled by family problems, fear of interruption or fear of pregnancy. Sex may not reach such peaks as before—but neither do they reach such troughs of personal anxiety or insecurity about themselves, their marriage or their sex life.

Sex and aging

As our youngsters become adults—and perhaps as our own parents are ill or dying—we begin to cast ourselves in the role of the family's elder statesmen, and for some this may imply putting away childish things such as sex, which is reserved for the young and beautiful. This is indeed sad, as sexual intimacy can continue to be an important and valuable part of an aging couple's relationship for as long as *they* mutually choose, if they can discard such stereotyped commercial views of sexuality and youth. Other aging couples abandon sexual expression of their love, but live happily and comfortably together. Problems especially arise if one of the pair *feels* more elderly than the other, and much careful discussion and negotiation may be needed to help the sexual peace.

If one ceases to be interested in sex the partner must learn to come to terms with the new state of affairs; and remember, it is not always the *man* who is left without sexual interest late in life. Individuals vary enormously in how they resolve the issue of unrequited sexual feelings. Many people, denied sexual outlet, find their own sexual appetite diminishes with time. Others seek extra-marital relationships, but the majority will masturbate, either in secret or with their partner, to relieve their sexual frustration. Some partners find this unacceptable or distasteful and may feel a mixture of anger and guilt that they are no longer sexually interested in their mate. A few sexually uninterested people continue to caress their partners to climax even though they gain no particular pleasure from the experience, other than seeing their partner's pleasure. Each couple must find their own way out of the problem of one-sided sex in as mutually acceptable a way as possible.

Sexual adjustment after bereavement is often a strain. The sudden death of a husband or wife when a couple are still sexually active may leave the remaining spouse with sexual frustration as well as grief. I have known older widows and widowers feel extremely guilty about starting to masturbate again after the death of their spouse—perhaps for the first time since adolescence. Such guilt may even prolong their grief and depression, which is such a pity. Masturbation is a perfectly harmless activity and often provides much solace and relief to lonely or unhappy people. In fact it might be said, without fear of exaggeration, that adjusting to our sexual relationship continues up to and even beyond our partner's death.

6 Homosexuality

I am continually surprised how deeply ingrained are the negative
attitudes towards homosexuality in our society as a whole. Yet, when
such attitudes are challenged, people usually come to see them as
emotional gut-reactions rather than anything they have sat down and
thought through. Paradoxically, amongst our most popular entertainers
are people who flaunt their homosexuality in a 'camp' fashion; perhaps
this allows the rest of the world to pigeon-hole them as 'queers',
'poofs', 'gays'—people totally unlike ourselves and laughable (or
disgusting). But the camp, effeminate theatrical homosexual does not
represent a typical male homosexual any more than an exaggerated
flirtatious sex-siren female represents a heterosexual, or a butch
woman, a lesbian. Nor does a homosexual prostitute or homosexual
sexual chancer represent homosexuality any more than a heterosexual
prostitute or a person out for casual sex represents heterosexuality.
Yet these are the homosexuals we tend to use for type-casting our
image of homosexuality. The public also have a confused view about
paedophilia (sexual exploitation of an under-age person by an adult) as
being exclusively homosexual, whereas the number of heterosexual
men who molest young girls is *far* greater than any homosexual
behaviour with underage boys.

The average homosexual man or woman is a normal person—in
height, build, weight, personality, background, career, social class and
ethnic group. Anyone might be a homosexual, that is preferring social
and sexual intimacy with persons of the *same* sex rather than the
opposite sex. An American study showed that up to 37 per cent of the
male population have had at least one homosexual experience, that 10
per cent of men have had considerable homosexual experience and
that 4 per cent of men are exclusively homosexual. This last figure is
thought to be similar in Britain. The figures for lesbians (homosexual
women) are lower and approximately 1 per cent of women are
exclusively lesbian.

No one has yet produced a convincing explanation about why some
people are heterosexual, others homosexual and a few bisexual
(enjoying either homosexual or heterosexual relationships). Many
theories abound, however: abnormal relationships in childhood with

father or mother (not proven); abnormal hormonal influences on a baby before birth (possible but not proven); single-sex schools (may encourage homosexuality but do not cause it); fear of heterosexuality (may be true in a proportion of homosexuals); prevailing social attitudes and values (may be true for some lesbians who, because of the women's liberation movement, do not want to see themselves as receptacles for men). Childhood histories give us no clues and neither do current personalities. Apart from the shared problems of social discrimination, homosexual men and women have no common denominator.

If we are *all* inherently bisexual, and only see ourselves as heterosexual because of our early sex-role stereotyping by family, friends and media, then it is difficult to explain why some people swim against the tide of social convention. Personally, I can only interpret this as an inherent biological and emotional homosexual drive that is at least as powerful as the heterosexual drive—and probably more so, in that it forces a person into the discomfort of a minority group almost despite themselves. I most certainly do *not* see it as sick or wrong, but as an alternative form of sexual expression, just as understandable (and statistically deviant) as celibacy, singleness or voluntary childlessness.

Although homosexual men and women share the problem of social discrimination they also have significant differences. Two women living together face less social disapproval and less suspicion about their private sexual life than men. Even if they held hands or cuddled in public, few would notice or be offended. And, unlike men, they can become single parents without risk of social outrage (unless they wish to adopt a child, when they will face the same problems as the male homosexual pair). Lesbians are no more likely to be masculine women than male homosexuals camp. Some lesbians are undoubtedly feminist—but not all feminists are lesbians.

Lesbian women describe the benefits of a same-sex relationship as having deeper levels of affection and understanding, more mutual support and openness of communication, and more emotional expression and freedom from the sex-role stereotypes than they get from heterosexual relationships. In some homosexual relationships, however (both male and female), one partner may choose to take a more passive 'feminine' role with the other partner in a more dominant and 'masculine' position.

Homosexuality

Let us now look at some of the problems facing the sexual awakening of homosexual teenagers and their families. Although I will do this mainly with reference to *him*, remember that a female homosexual will go through many of the same anxieties as a male.

Many boys pass through a period in adolescence when they experiment in sexual games with the same sex—especially in residential settings. Some girls develop a teenage crush on a school friend or woman teacher—romantically besotted with a person of the same sex, before transferring their attention at a later stage to a young man. But a proportion of youngsters begin to realise that they are not like the others. Their sexual thoughts and fantasies are fixed and predictably directed towards people of the same sex. Let's look at a typical homosexual youngster, who begins to recognise that whereas his friends are sharing erotic feelings towards girls, he is not.

As he will have grown up in the same world as the others, his 'gut' views about the possibility of being a homosexual will be the same as everyone else's: poofters, queers. Yet, horror of horrors, he is feeling attracted to men and must be one of 'them' too. It is hard to imagine the anxiety and confusion produced by such self-revelation. Most teenagers facing this identity confusion become socially withdrawn and isolated in their misery. They dread that their fears become known to others who, they rightly predict, would at best not know how to cope with their suspicions and at worst reject, ridicule or punish them for such ideas. Some feel so awful they reject sexual expression for life; others attempt suicide. (If society scorns you, you tend to scorn yourself.) Some attempt to deny their homosexual drive and force themselves 'cold' into heterosexual relationships, and even marriage and parenthood, to beat the spectre of homosexuality that haunts them. Some cause considerable unhappiness to their families by declaring their homosexuality much later in adult life.

But most slowly accommodate and adjust to the idea that they are different from their friends, and gradually drift away from them to a homosexual peer-group, if they are fortunate to live near a large town. A homosexual may take many years to go through this so-called 'coming out' process—from acknowledging his homosexuality to becoming sexually active, to telling friends and family and to acknowledging his homosexuality publicly or politically (the last two stages may never occur).

Coping with Sexual Relationships

The process of personal accommodation and adjustment to homosexuality often occurs in the setting of a stormy rejection of the teenager by his or her parents. Most teenagers embarking on their early sexual adventures face parental disapproval or criticism, but that pales into insignificance compared with parents' reactions to any hint of homosexuality from their youngster. Why should this be so? The parents are not only grappling with the *public's* negative attitudes towards homosexuality which they probably share (just as their son or daughter did); they also have their own *private* emotional problems about homosexuality too. These will include guilt feelings that they must have failed somehow as parents, anger that their child could cause such humiliation to them (what will the neighbours think), sorrow at the loss of their conventional future—marriage, grand-children—and confusion about the reality of him or her appearing still to look the same (and behave the same towards them) yet be one of 'those'!

A few parents manage to work through this chaos of emotions, perhaps by sharing their grief with a sensitive doctor or relatives or a gay counselling agency, and eventually come to terms with the loss of some of their original ambitions for their son or daughter, and can re-establish their relationship with their youngster as something permanent and independent of the vagaries of his or her private sex life (a similar process, in fact, to that gone through by parents of heterosexuals). Family tensions over a son's homosexuality may lead to rifts between father and mother or elder sister, with Dad openly rejecting his son and Mum or elder sister secretly keeping in touch. In fact, homosexuals need as much support and acceptance from their families as they can get, to cope with the victimisation they will experience in their lives, which can take many forms.

Homosexuals may be excluded from certain work-roles—for example residential care establishments, school teaching, social work, public office—although the reasoning is somewhat obscure. Certainly a homosexual is no more likely to molest or rape a youngster than a hetero-sexual—rather less so, in fact. Men often describe feeling threatened by a homosexual in their presence and this 'fear of rape' is so foreign to a man that he overreacts by victimisation. Most heterosexuals fear we may give the wrong impression to a homosexual—that we may inadvertently be flirting, but don't recognise the ground rules with our own sex—and that may contribute to our unease too. Homosexuals rarely become attracted to people who are basically heterosexual, and such fears are totally unfounded. Although homosexuals will perceive the 'I'm not interested' messages as quickly as heterosexuals, they sadly have to cope with more hurtful messages of social rejection too as they are deemed by some unfit for civilised company.

As a result, homosexuals tend not to declare their homosexuality at work or with their 'straight' friends. Maintaining the secret becomes a stress in its own right. Alternatively, they may declare their homosexuality but protect themselves by living in an exclusively gay community, frequenting gay bars and only risking work in a setting where gay people are accepted without question. As with other minority groups who feel under threat from the majority, they tend to join together for mutual support, and many gay groups now exist. Gay groups, gay newspapers and gay counsellors have generally improved the opportunities for people grappling with the issues of homosexuality whether privately or publicly—and the law, the church, the press and most professional groups are beginning to acquire a more acceptable and accepting attitude to this once illegal behaviour.

Finally—a glimpse at the problems of homosexual sexual behaviour. Homosexuals have to learn their 'rules of conduct' in sexual relationships from their peer group in the same haphazard way as heterosexuals. They have even less sex education that is relevant. Homosexual sexuality has the same uses and abuses as heterosexuality (see Chapter 1). It can be a source of pleasure or a relief of tension; it can establish intimacy and close relationships, bolster self-esteem and a sense of masculinity or femininity, and may be used to hold power over another person. But homosexual relationships differ significantly from heterosexual relationships in several respects. Sociologists consider it may be the woman who preserves the monogamy and longevity of heterosexual relationships and that, left to their own devices, men would be serially monogamous (going from one woman to another over time) or polygamous. Without a woman, they argue, homosexual male pairings tend to be shorter-lasting—although periods of stable relationships are still common, with the same degree of warmth and emotional involvement as experienced by heterosexual couples. Lesbians tend to have longer and more stable relationships but even so, the average duration is about three years. Homosexual men are also more prone to enjoying casual sexual encounters than heterosexuals, again perhaps because there is not a woman involved (she would be more likely to encourage emotional involvement and commitment).

Because homosexual relationships are conducted under considerable social pressure and often in a clandestine fashion, they are less secure. They lack the social approval and public commitment that legal marital status provides. Sexual jealousy and fear of abandonment is more likely than in heterosexual couples. Lesbians and homosexual male couples tend to continue mixing with their single friends at gay bars, etc., and thus have less exclusive relationships than heterosexual couples and more likelihood of changing affiliation.

Male and female homosexual couples experience the same sort of emotional ups and downs as heterosexual people and have particular problems when under stress such as illness, hospitalisation or death, when they may be unable to reveal their personal concern and emotional commitment in public at a time of great personal distress. Like all people in close relationships, they may suffer from excessive hopes and false expectations, and have the same problems in balancing personal space and intimacy as all other relationships. Lesbians sometimes become tremendously interdependent and identified with each other, risking great emotional heights and depths as a result.

Homosexual sexual problems are no different from heterosexual ones. There may be problems with erection or orgasm, with responsiveness or loss of sexual appetite. These might be caused by the same factors that produce heterosexual problems—relationship problems, sexual inhibitions from childhood, anxiety about infection, distaste for oral sex or internal conflict about homosexuality.

Homosexual pairs lack the anchoring effect of children, although stable homosexual pairs (both lesbian and male homosexual) are beginning to challenge the assumption that they are not fit to be natural or adoptive parents. Research in America suggests that homosexual parents are as effective as heterosexual parents both in looking after children, and in promoting a child's normal sexual development, and underline that most homosexuals are the product of heterosexual parents. The lack of an opposite-sex parent figure is no different in a single-parent family, and children of a homosexual couple usually accept the atypical nature of their domestic arrangements without difficulty. Nevertheless, being a single parent and a lesbian means a double social stigma, which must put great pressure on such families—especially if the child's grandparents have rejected their daughter as a lesbian. It is my experience that a child may accept the revelation of a parent's homosexuality with less difficulty than a parent can accept homosexuality in a teenager.

But a wife or husband, confronted with news that their spouse is homosexual, and has a same-sex lover, may be totally devastated. A wife may doubt her own femininity and attractiveness as a result, feel betrayed or used as a vehicle to satisfy his social status or his need to be a parent rather than a husband. She will feel unable to compete with his lover and trapped in her mortification and rejection, unable to share her misery with her closest friend or relatives. A husband may feel similarly humiliated by his wife's declaration of her lesbianism. After a spouse has declared his or her homosexuality a couple may face an enormous dilemma about whether to stay together or not. Great affection may exist between them and in some cases their marital sexual relationship may continue, despite the knowledge of homosexual encounters. More commonly the partners lose all interest in sex and the relationship continues simply to preserve a social front for the children's sake. Or it may end—leaving both partners with the onerous decision of deciding whether or not to declare the reasons for the split. The hurt and humiliated spouse may, in anger and desire for retribution, reveal the partner's defection to homosexuality and then regret this at a later stage, or may keep the secret hidden because of fear of the questions it might raise about his or her own sexual capacity.

In concluding this chapter, we should perhaps consider the very positive aspects of homosexuality. Same-sex relationships seem less bound by social conventions, expectations and stereotypes. If a homosexual couple choose to stay together, it is from personal choice rather than from social or legal pressure. Once together, they are less likely to fall into the traditional assumption about who does what in their relationship. The 'husband and wife' or 'man and woman' job descriptions are avoided, and they are more likely to relate as person to person, on equal terms. Even more important, they are more likely to be sensitive to each other's needs because of their same-sex identification and sympathy. To achieve similar understanding in a heterosexual couple requires considerable motivation, understanding and good communication. Perhaps because of this shared identification, homosexuals sometimes seem more willing to allow a greater freedom for sexual expression and sensuality in their lives. So all of us, whether homosexual or heterosexual, can learn a great deal about relationships in general from what is best in same-sex relationships.

7 Normal Sexual Responses and Common Problems

If you are uncomfortable or inhibited about sex, or if you have a particular sex problem, this and the next chapter may help you resolve it. It will be more effective if you can persuade your partner to read and discuss it with you, and most effective of all if you can carry out some of the practical ideas suggested in Chapter 8.

The importance of sexual pleasure in our lives is a matter of personal choice. Its significance varies enormously over a lifetime, and may decrease as our interests and opportunities widen, and as our sexual experiences mellow from frenetic excitement to the comfortable predictability of a long-term relationship. It is perfectly possible to lead a happy and contented married life with no sexual activity, with diminished sexual responses, infrequent intercourse, or relying on mutual caressing short of intercourse for sexual pleasure. No one is watching you or your responses except yourselves. If you are both happy with the status quo of your sex life—then you do *not* have a sexual problem. Nevertheless, you may still learn something to your advantage by reading the rest of this chapter and the next!

Although sexual behaviour is extremely variable and idiosyncratic, there are certain predictable sexual responses that our body is capable of—and it is the failure or fear of failure of these desired responses that give us our sexual hang-ups and problems.

Sexual responses

Once adult, our body becomes capable of sexual function—whether we like the idea or not. We acquire a sexual appetite or libido and an ability to have sexual responses even if we live alone and never make use of them. We need to understand these responses.

Sexual appetite

Our interest, or libido, varies not only from person to person but in the same individual too, according to circumstances, age and—in women—the menstrual cycle. Our sexual appetite (and responses) can be stimulated in a congenial setting, for example on holiday; by the novelty of a new relationship; by alcohol (in moderation); and by things that make us feel good about ourselves, such as new clothes, success, slimming, another's approval. But it is particularly susceptible to the emotional climate of our sexual relationship, so that even a hint of anger or resentment or anxiety can be enough to switch off sexual desire—fortunately only temporarily, if we can resolve the disturbance in the climate!

Boredom, ill-health or tiredness and feelings of depression and self-depreciation don't help our sexual appetite either. And people who think sex is disgusting or wrong may be preoccupied with sex but rarely experience sexual desire in a real relationship—it would be too confusing for their value system. The average frequency of intercourse for married couples is 2·4 times per week—but this is a useless and misleading figure, as it encompasses those who enjoy sex once per month and those who need it once a day. Only you can decide what frequency seems acceptable for you *both*.

Sexual arousal

We can become sexually aroused simply by thinking or having fantasies about sex or, more commonly, by a combination of fantasies and physical stimulation. Provided that we are in the mood, want to respond, feel relaxed and accepting of ourself, our partner and our surroundings, and—most important—that we have appropriate stimulation, sexual arousal should occur quite naturally.

Typical behaviour that leads to sexual arousal can include kissing, cuddling and caressing by another or by yourself (masturbation). Certain areas of our body are more sensitive to touch such as lips, breasts, inner thigh and genitals, and caressing of these areas is more likely to lead to arousal. Some people find oral sex (kissing each other's genitalia) to be arousing—others find it distasteful and a sexual turn-off. In fact, each couple must work out for themselves what they find stimulating and acceptable behaviour: what feels good one day may tickle or feel uncomfortable the next—be prepared to experiment and be prepared to tell each other what you fancy, and what you don't like. Don't stick to preconceived notions—they can be very wrong!

During sexual arousal, both men and women experience psychological feelings of excitement, accompanied by physical changes such as increased heart rate, rapid breathing, muscle tension, sweating, and some blushing of face and neck. Men develop an erection of the penis, which is caused by an increase of blood flowing in and less flowing out, as valves in the penile vein close.

Women have a similar increase in blood flow to their genital region, and this causes a slight swelling of the inner lips and entrance to their vagina, and the production of moisture, or lubrication, from the vaginal walls. The upper or inner part of the vagina balloons out as arousal increases, so that only the lower third of the vagina remains in close contact with the penis during intercourse. It is also the only part of the vagina that can feel touch. This is an important fact because many men worry that their penis may be too small to satisfy a woman. The cervix, or neck of the womb, rises slightly into the abdomen during sexual arousal, so that if a woman has vaginal intercourse before she is fully aroused both the low-lying cervix and the lack of lubrication may cause her to have discomfort or pain. This is called dyspareunia.

Orgasm or climax

Once sexual arousal has reached a peak, if appropriate stimulation continues, then orgasm may occur. This is a sudden release of muscle tension accompanied by rhythmic contractions of the pelvic muscle (and the uterus in women). In men it is associated with ejaculation of semen, which is like saliva but contains sperm. It is perfectly clean and harmless—but can cause pregnancy! During orgasm, the subjective feelings of excitement and pleasure are at their most intense.

Most women need stimulation of their clitoris (a knob of sensitive tissue in front of the vaginal opening) as well as vaginal intercourse in order to reach a climax. This is normal. No recognisable difference has been shown between orgasms achieved by intercourse or by caressing, although they may feel different in intensity. Some women report having a particularly sensitive area on the front wall of their vagina which has been called the G spot—but such an area has never been demonstrated scientifically.

Resolution phase

This is the 'lull after the storm', when the body settles down and both partners feel fulfilled and calm, often pleasantly sleepy and relaxed. In the woman the feeling of fullness or congestion in her pelvis and her general sense of excitement may take longer to settle, particularly if she has not experienced a climax. A man usually has a short 'latent period' after climax, during which he cannot obtain another erection. The length of the latent period increases as a man gets older.

Common sexual problems

Most of us experience difficulty in achieving the sort of sexual response we would like to have, some of the time—and some of us have difficulties with our sexual responses most of the time. If the latter is the case, we have a sexual problem. Sexual problems do not occur in isolation, but usually in the context of a relationship (although we may experience them in masturbation too). Often both partners in a marriage will have sexual problems—for example, he may have premature ejaculation and she may have lost interest in sex. But even if only one partner appears to have the sexual problem (e.g. difficulty with orgasms), they *both* have a sexual problem. There is no such thing as an uninvolved sexual partner. The anxiety that is produced by one or other failing to respond may be so intense that it invades their lovemaking and perpetuates what might otherwise have been a trivial passing difficulty.

Typical male sexual problems

Loss of interest in sex (loss of libido, desire or appetite)

If a man loses interest, it tends to upset a couple's sex life more than if the woman's libido is reduced, because men more commonly initiate love-making. Sometimes a man will still enjoy sex once it has begun, even though he has no interest at the beginning.

Poor erections (impotence)

There are difficulties in describing erections, but most men know when they have a full erection, and complain of partial, incomplete or absent erections which are insufficient to enable intercourse to occur. Usually the man can achieve an erection when alone or spontaneously when he awakes, but finds he cannot have one with his partner when he chooses.

Loss of sexual pleasure

A man may experience a normal erection and ejaculate normally, but feel no enjoyment or psychological arousal associated with love-making.

Problems with ejaculation

Premature ejaculation. A man is said to have premature ejaculation if he ejaculates sooner than he or his partner would choose. Most men start their sex lives with poor control over when they ejaculate, but gradually learn to delay their climax until their partner feels ready. Some men ejaculate even before they have a full erection.

Delayed ejaculation. Failure to ejaculate may not be a problem until a couple wish to have children, when they may appear at the infertility clinic rather than the sexual problems clinic. Some men can ejaculate with masturbation but not inside their partner's vagina; others will only have experienced ejaculation when asleep as a nocturnal emission or 'wet dream'.

Retrograde ejaculation. This sometimes occurs after a man has had a prostate operation. His sexual responses are perfectly normal and he reaches climax as usual; but during emission of the semen, due to damage to valves near the bladder neck, the semen discharges into the bladder rather than out of the penis. It cannot be corrected, but most couples learn to accept the new state of affairs.

Typical female sexual problems

Loss of libido (sexual interest)

This is a common problem, especially after childbirth and when suffering from depression, and leads to the classic 'I'm too tired' or 'I've got a headache' clichés. Women's libido is thought to be similar to men's, but it is prone to greater variation due to the regular monthly hormonal changes.

Poor responsiveness (frigidity)

If a woman fails to respond sexually, she may complain of pain with intercourse (dyspareunia), due to poor lubrication and low-lying cervix.

Lack of orgasm

A woman may never have experienced an orgasm (this is called being pre-orgasmic), or may have lost the ability to have them with her partner, whether or not she continues to achieve orgasm by masturbation. Anxiety in a man tends to bring forward the time of his climax (premature ejaculation) and delay a woman's, perhaps indefinitely.

Loss of sexual enjoyment

Some women, although continuing to respond genitally, record feeling 'dead from the neck down' and gain no pleasure from arousal or orgasm. They may find the idea of sex repels them as a result.

Non-consummation (vaginismus)

This problem is different from the rest. A woman may respond sexually in normal fashion—she may have a normal interest in sex, become aroused and reach a climax—but may not allow vaginal intercourse to occur. Her vaginal muscles tighten into spasm, so that not even her partner's finger is allowed inside, and she will experience great fear if any attempt is made to penetrate.

Abnormal sexual behaviour

For completeness, we should include the rarer types of sexual problems because they can sometimes interfere with the sexual relationship of a couple. Some of them make newspaper headlines because they are rightly illegal. Most, although not all, are male problems. A complete discussion of them lies outside the scope of the book.

Transvestism—the desire to dress in clothes of the opposite sex. A transvestite is not usually a homosexual, although homosexual men do occasionally dress in 'drag' to attract their partner. Transvestite men are often heterosexual and married. They may obtain sexual gratification by dressing in women's clothes, or may act in this way in response to an obsessional drive, feeling temporarily more relaxed and at peace in a feminine garb and image. Such behaviour is likely to cause considerable distress and embarrassment to his family, and may interfere with his marital sexual relationship. In the appendix is a contact address for transvestites or their families.

Trans-sexuality. This is a problem of gender identity, and occurs when an individual, either man or woman, becomes convinced he or she is in a body of the wrong sex. They feel and want to behave like a person of the opposite sex. They feel attracted to people of the same sex, not as a homosexual but believing they are heterosexual. It is a rare condition and usually becomes apparent in young adulthood; but occasionally a person does not reveal his trans-sexual ideas until later, perhaps after marriage and having a family, when the revelation of this desire to reverse sex can have a profoundly upsetting effect on family and marital life.

Sexual fetishistic behaviour. Some people use strange or highly abnormal methods to stimulate themselves sexually; some of these need cause no offence, but others can be off-putting for their sexual partner. Some need bizarre clothing, a fantasy setting, sexual rituals, the use of violence—to themselves (masochism) or to others (sadism)—or other idiosyncratic practices. Some relationships can come to terms with the bizarre nature of one partner's sexual needs; but if they intrude on the other's sexual relaxation and pleasure, then a negotiated compromise must be reached. Such practices are usually requested by men, who can cause their wives the great anguish of choosing whether to collude with their wishes or take a firm stand against them. Prostitutes often report that they provide a service for such bizarre practices, which other women are not prepared to condone. Many theories about harsh and primitive upbringings are used to explain sado-masochistic behaviour, but this is difficult to prove. If this is a problem in your relationship, I suggest that you both discuss it openly and try some agreed series of limited caressing in a relaxed setting. This will encourage your natural sexual responses to occur free from anxiety and the demands of intercourse. Talk to each other about your feelings and needs. Violence during love-making is a contradiction in terms; it is both dangerous and undesirable, and should be condoned by no one.

Voyeurism. This is a particular form of sexual fetish in which a person obtains sexual gratification from the secret and illicit watching of other people in compromising situations (making love, undressing or going to the toilet, for example).

Exhibitionism. The exposure of a man's genitals in a public setting. It is usually directed towards an unknown woman in order to disturb her. Exhibitionists may feel insecure or inadequate about their sexual capacity or competence, and gain reassurance from the woman's reaction to them.

Paedophilia. Sexual behaviour between an adult and an under-age (less than sixteen) child. Although commonly assumed to describe a man behaving indecently with a young boy, it is in fact more commonly a man with an under-age girl. It is somewhat ironic that homosexuals, who are no more likely to be paedophiliacs than heterosexuals, are discouraged from teaching or social work, whereas heterosexuals are assumed to be safe!

Rape. Enforced sexual behaviour—usually by a man on a woman (although a few cases of females raping men have been recorded in America). It is usually associated with feelings of aggression towards women, and is a particularly emotionally violent form of physical assault, leaving destructive effects for a considerable period of time afterwards. A recent law has been adopted making rape within marriage a punishable offence. (See appendix for contact address for rape victims.)

Incest. Sexual behaviour between close family members—most commonly father or uncle and under-age daughter. This is not only an illegal and immoral act, but it may also lead to long-term difficulties in the sexual adjustment of the child thereafter, as well as causing serious marital problems between the adults should her mother find out. Often the child keeps her secret out of fear of father's reaction, or mother's reaction, or what effect the revelation will have on family unity (a massive responsibility on young shoulders); or she keeps her secret because of personal guilt or shame (youngsters readily assume they are to blame for everything that goes wrong), or out of ignorance that such behaviour is abnormal. We may only hear about incest when an adult, seeking help with sexual problems, reveals her own incestuous childhood for the first time.

Although incest represents a total violation of trust and dependency between child and adult, it is becoming possible for counsellors to work with such families in confidence without the legal process having to remove the offender to prison (which may disrupt the child's life more than the incest itself). If such problems exist in your family—please seek help urgently.

8 A Self-Help Approach to Sexual Problems

In order to tackle your own particular sexual difficulties or hang-ups, it is important to deal with three important areas.

1 *Why sexual problems arise*

There are a whole range of reasons or background causes which can lead to problems with responses, or to loss of interest in sex. You may find that some of those mentioned below are relevant to you; they need to be dealt with if your sex life is to improve. Tackling the cause of a sexual problem usually needs the co-operation of two people, so if you can persuade your partner to read this chapter too, you are much more likely to benefit.

2 *Sexual performance anxiety*

This perpetuates a sexual problem long after the original cause may have disappeared. Both partners lose confidence in their performance, and instead of relaxing they start to watch their sexual responses like 'spectators', rather than being involved in what is going on. And of course, the more you watch for responses, the less you respond. This can become a cause of sexual problems in its own right. The best way to tackle this is, for a temporary period, to reduce your sexual aims and objectives into small and manageable steps; we have called these stages I to IV.

These steps are important not only in reducing your sexual anxiety, but also in helping you to come face to face with the underlying background factors which caused the sexual problem in the first place. Often our sexual inhibitions or angry feelings towards our partner are only revealed when we try simply to caress him or her and find that we feel a strong revulsion or resistance to doing so. It is the examination of that resistance that tells you what your problem is all about; so don't underestimate the importance of the early stages I and II—that is when you learn about yourselves, and (I hope) learn to communicate with each other.

3 *Special techniques*

These may be necessary for particular sexual problems such as premature ejaculation or vaginismus; but remember that it is no use looking for 'cures' unless you have tried to understand why your particular problem has arisen.

To sum up: to deal with your sexual problems you must cope with background causes, sexual anxiety and specific techniques—a package deal that provides a challenging but interesting journey which, if successful, should lead to a more fulfilled and satisfactory sex life.

Causes of sexual problems

Sex is a natural function like digestion—and, like digestion, it can be upset by a whole variety of problems, other than physical illness. We all accept that faulty eating, feeling rushed, stressed, anxious or in a bad mood can lead to complaints like loss of appetite, indigestion, diarrhoea or constipation, even though the body is basically healthy. We also know that if we eat normally and in a relaxed way, our digestive system works naturally by itself. In a similar way, if we allow ourselves to accept physical stimulation in a relaxed and unhurried way, our bodies will respond sexually without any conscious effort on our part.

There are certain background factors which tend to interfere with our relaxation and acceptance of sexual contact, and it is these factors that cause our failure to respond. You may recognise some of them as being present in your own experiences. If you are uneasy or unresponding in *your* sexual relationship, they may be significant for you. Before I list these general causes of sexual problems, I should emphasise one complex but highly important point. The same sexual problem can be caused by a whole variety of different background problems, and the same background problem (e.g. guilt) can cause a whole variety of sexual problems (e.g. problems with erections, orgasm, vaginismus, etc.). There is no direct correlation between the sort of symptoms and the background cause. So, whatever your particular sexual problem may be, you must look at the list of possible background causes to see which is most relevant for you—and don't be too surprised if you find they are all relevant!

- Physical or medical problem (rare)
- Ignorance or misunderstanding about sex
- Problems in your relationship
- Bad feelings about yourself or your body
- Guilt feelings and inhibitions about sex
- Unsuitable circumstances

I have produced that rather bald list to give you an idea of the wide range of background reasons for the development of sexual difficulties. I hope it emphasises why it is not possible to give a simple 'recipe book' formula for curing any particular problem.

How to tackle the background causes

Physical and medical problems

Although sexual problems are not commonly caused by medical complaints, if you experience pain, soreness or bleeding with intercourse, or if you are a young man having no erections whatsoever, you should ask your family doctor for a check-up to exclude diabetes, genital infections or other medical causes. Vaginal infections are a common cause of sexual problems, and can easily be treated. If you cannot consummate your relationship, you should also seek medical advice—perhaps asking a woman doctor to examine you.

Drugs for high blood pressure, depression or arthritis can sometimes upset your sexual responses, so check with your doctor if a sexual problem has developed while taking such drugs. Remember, too, that excess alcohol, chronic tiredness, recent illness, and being generally unfit may impair your sexual interest and responses, and that restoring yourself to good physical health may be all that is necessary for a return of your responsiveness. If you have had a recent operation or illness, remember that it is better to have limited caressing short of intercourse rather than no physical contact at all. This is especially so after disfiguring surgery or after a coronary, when confidence and morale are low (see Chapter 4).

Family doctors can give full contraceptive advice to anyone of the age of sixteen, and if you feel anxious or unsure about anything related to sex or contraception your doctor or local family planning clinic should be able to help. Try to choose the contraceptive method that fits your life-style and sex life most effectively.

If you are physically handicapped, don't feel embarrassed about asking for contraceptive advice at home. The physically disabled are just as entitled to a sex life as anyone else.

Ignorance and misunderstanding about sex

If we are unsure about what to do and what to expect from sex, we become anxious and no longer obey our instincts (which are to relax and enjoy what is happening). We may worry unnecessarily about pregnancy or pain, or we may fear that if we let ourselves go we will become undignified, animal-like or unattractive. Some women fear that if they relax and become aroused to orgasm they will be incontinent of urine (this is exceedingly rare). Some of these fears can only be resolved by experience, but others can be relieved by sharing them with your partner, with a friend, or by checking with your doctor or at the family planning clinic. A simple book about sexual anatomy might help too.

There are some common misunderstandings about our sexual responses that I would like to share with you—using a simple graph of sexual responses as a 'map'.

1 *Sexual appetite.* It is possible to enjoy love-making even though you didn't feel in the mood at first. Many couples, after they have been married for a while, lose their appetite and assume that they should stop making love as a result. Try sometimes having sex to please your partner—you may be surprised at how much you enjoy it, after all! The less sex you have, the less you seem to want, so don't wind down too much if you want your sex life to continue.

2 *Erection.* A man's penis can become erect at an early stage in sexual arousal, especially in a young man. This does not mean that he is necessarily aroused enough for intercourse, and he may start penetration far too soon—before his partner feels ready. She may become anxious because she feels she is keeping him waiting and collude with rushing ahead, pretending to be aroused. It is much better to kiss and caress for a time first (foreplay).

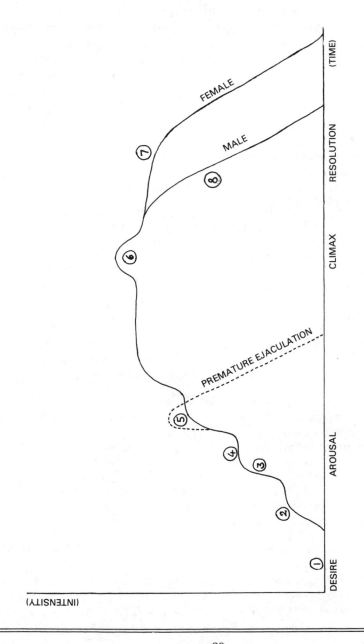

Sexual Response Curve

3 *Vaginal lubrication.* The moisture being produced may remain hidden inside the vagina, especially when the woman is lying down. Both partners may assume she is not responding when in fact she is. Remember that the penis gives a more obvious signal of response than the vagina—which means a man cannot pretend to be aroused!

4 *Arousal comes in waves.* Both the man and the woman may find that their arousal comes and goes, with increasing and decreasing erections and vaginal responses. This is quite normal. A decline does not mean something is wrong, so try not to develop 'performance anxiety'. Just have a rest for a moment; then carry on caressing each other until your responses return.

5 *Premature ejaculation.* 'Coming' too soon (i.e. before either partner wants to) is normal for young men, particularly when very sexually aroused, and when there has been a long interval since the last ejaculation. You have to learn to control it. Too rapid ejaculation can make a woman worry that she will take too long to reach her climax; this may cause her to 'switch off', or not to switch on at all, if it is a regular occurrence when you make love. This is a common problem, yet one which most couples find extremely difficult to talk about with each other. If you or your partner have this problem, try to discuss it together in a friendly way and see if you can improve the situation by following the suggestions given later in this chapter.

6 *Orgasm.* Many women never have an orgasm, yet are otherwise fully responsive sexually. This does not mean that they are 'frigid'. In most early sexual relationships orgasms for the woman are unusual—yet both partners may become extremely anxious about this. Some women pretend to have orgasms to please their partners. The more a man demands an orgasm from his partner, the less likely he is to get one. She needs to feel relaxed, trusting and free from pressure. Whereas 'performance anxiety' makes the man come more quickly, it has the opposite effect on a woman. There is no need for her to experience an orgasm every time. She will be more likely to have an orgasm if she is caressed gently on her clitoris. She should show her partner what feels nice.

For both men and women, the ability to become aroused sexually, and the intensity of orgasm, may be much greater during masturbation than when making love with their partner. This may worry some people; but it is not surprising, because our own 'biofeedback' system is much better than our partner's ability to understand our physical needs at a particular moment. Nevertheless, most people feel that the psychological and emotional heights of intimacy with another far outweigh the physiological heights of masturbation. During the experience of orgasm, most people become slightly 'detached' from their partner for a short time.

7 *Resolution (the woman).* A woman may take longer to 'come down' from sexual arousal than a man, whether or not she has reached a climax. This means that she may wish for more caressing or hugging.

8 *Resolution (the man).* He, on the other hand, may be snoring within one minute of ejaculation! This may produce resentment if his wife is still feeling the need for intimacy. Wake him up sometimes, and let him sleep at other times. That way, you both get what you want some of the time.

Problems in your relationship

In the earlier part of this book—particularly Chapters 3 and 5—I have looked at the common problem areas that lead to resentment and anger in even the best regulated relationships. Differences of opinion are not a problem within marriage if they can be aired, mulled over, negotiated and settled. But if a couple cannot communicate comfortably with each other, then differences of opinion remain unresolved and soon grow into resentment which can invade the most loving relationship, having dire consequences on sexual expression and response. Therefore we must look at the issues of good communication in some detail. I urge you to read this whether or not you have a sexual problem,

It is never too late to learn new ways of communication, however long you have been together, and in my experience improved communication is essential if a sexual problem is to be resolved. Here are some basic principles of communication:

Aim to communicate with each other as two adults. In many marriages the husband communicates like a father and the wife like a child . . . and in others the wife behaves like a mother to her husband, who reacts like a son. Such 'parent and child' relationships do not promote or encourage healthy adult sexual responsiveness. The following points help to keep the status equal.

Self-expression. Teach yourself to 'self-assert' and 'self-protect' by using the expression 'I would like . . .' or 'I feel hurt because . . .' instead of the more traditional 'Should we . . .', 'Why don't you . . .' or 'If only you . . .'. The usual method of communication (often thought to be unselfish) is to think or guess what your partner would like, rather than revealing your own wishes. This pattern can be fraught with all sorts of problems—you may always have been guessing wrong, and your partner has never liked to tell you for fear of hurting you (being unselfish again), so that long-standing assumptions about what the other likes or dislikes may be quite incorrect. Or you may constantly be telling your partner what he or she should be doing differently (which is nagging).

A much safer and less complicated way to communicate is to express your own thoughts and feelings and ideas, and let your partner do the same thing. This keeps your own house in order by asserting and protecting yourself, and lets your partner do the same. If any change in behaviour is required, each partner does it from *choice* (having heard what the other would like), rather than because of nagging or coercion.

It is important to be able to express clearly *what you want* (self-assertion) and *what upsets you* (self-protection), ventilating angry feelings in as controlled and constructive a way as possible; destructive remarks do *not* help to resolve anger or resentment—they can just provoke a vicious circle of hostility. It is essential to concentrate on exploring *your* feelings, e.g. 'I feel upset when you don't talk to me', instead of telling your partner what to do, e.g. 'Why don't you speak to me?' (which is nagging). It is up to *your partner* to decide whether to change his or her behaviour in response to your statements—nagging is the least effective way to encourage change.

Listen to your partner. In exchange for you being able to express yourself, your partner must be encouraged to do the same. When listening, be careful not to over-react even if some comments may upset you; you are trying to encourage an *honest* exchange of *real* feelings and facts.

Negotiation. Once you have both declared your likes and dislikes, try to negotiate fairly so that each gives something and gains something. If one wants black and the other white, don't have grey; have black and white alternately. For example, if your husband likes to go to the pub with you, but you prefer to stay at home (but not on your own), then offer to go to the pub with him sometimes and hope that, in exchange, he will sometimes stay in with you.

Praise.   Aim to notice and remark on something that pleases you in your partner's behaviour at least once a day—I mean *both* of you, not just the men. We tend to assume that paying compliments is a male prerogative—it's not! Praise will change a person's behaviour far more effectively than criticism and nagging, but we have to work harder to notice the good things than the bad.

Bad feelings about yourself or your body

I looked at these in some detail in Chapters 4 and 5 in the context of illness and mid-life changes. The same principles apply whatever your health and age. If you don't like yourself or your body, you won't feel happy about someone else trying to get close to you. Self-acceptance is an important part of personal maturation. Instead of accepting those usual automatic stereotyped inner comments about yourself ('I won't bother to do that; it's only for me'), try talking to yourself as a parent: use some alternative ideas ('Well, why shouldn't I treat myself to a nice meal? I deserve it as much as anyone else!'). Stop trying to superimpose some perfect physical image on yourself so that by contrast you always fail—instead, look at your good points and advantages in their own right; you are the way nature planned you to be, so make the best of what you have instead of looking over your shoulder! A short jog or a few physical exercises can do wonders for the ego—and losing a few pounds in weight can, too.

Guilt feelings and inhibitions about sex

These are usually acquired during childhood, from our parents and those in authority above us. These are not so easy to deal with by yourself—but try! You are aiming to discard attitudes and values about sex you acquired as a child and reprocess them as an adult, realising how silly and mythical are some of the ideas people instilled in you when you were gullible. By now, you will no longer believe that babies appeared under gooseberry bushes—yet you may still believe that sex is disgusting and wrong! In that case, how have household names and famous people acquired children? They must have done the same things in their bedroom that you do in yours. Try looking at books like Alex Comfort's *The Joy of Sex*—which was in the best-seller list for years. Thousands of British people approved of that, and even libraries stocked it. Sex is a normal and essential part of life; it is not disgusting and dirty unless it is 'out of context'. Try to abandon your infantile views and gain a new perspective! Talking with friends may help.

You may have acquired your sexual inhibitions after being hurt by a relationship that went wrong. Don't 'shut up shop'; learn from your mistakes. You shouldn't make the same one again! You know more now. If you had a particularly traumatic experience, such as rape, incest or abortion, you may need to talk about your problems with another neutral person or counsellor rather than your sexual partner. That can often help to put a new perspective on your ideas.

Unsuitable circumstances

These need little discussion! If you are too tired, or rushed or fear the invasion of young children or the intrusive ears of teenagers there is usually a simple remedy. Please try to allow time for making love! It is amazing how couples programme sex out of their lives when they are busy, and then find time to ask for help when sexual problems develop! Our physical relationship needs regular servicing, as much as our general interaction does, if it is to flourish. It cannot be fitted into holidays and the odd night here and there! It is useless to be perpetually too tired, or needing to get up early, or worried about this and that. Question your priorities and find a slot for your sex life! A lock on the door—a radio by the bed—KY jelly at the ready—tissues—warmth—soft lights. You are not being self-indulgent if you organise such items; you are 'servicing' your relationship as you would your car!

Coping with sexual 'performance anxiety' and being a spectator

It is usually 'performance anxiety' that keeps a sexual problem going. The original resentment or difficulty may be long past, but the vicious circle of worrying about your responses continues. You start to watch your performance as a spectator, rather than being fully involved in it—and the more you watch, the less you respond. In addition, if one partner fails to respond, then the other partner gets caught up in 'performance anxiety' too, and doubts his or her abilities as a sexual partner. There is no such thing as an uninvolved partner, so don't make one of you the Patient and the other the Therapist—you are *both* involved in the problem.

Guidelines to reduce performance anxiety, help you to start responding, and improve your lovemaking

What follows should be considered in conjunction with what I have already said about communication, which is equally important for improving sexual relationships.

There are two important goals:

- Correct misunderstanding about sex—and show each other what you like.

- Learn ways to avoid the 'spectator' role and allow yourself to relax and enjoy your natural sexual responses. By setting limits to how far you go physically for an agreed time, this allows you to concentrate on and re-acquaint yourself with your body sensations with no goal in mind.

This approach is primarily educational: you are not curing an illness, but learning new and more satisfactory ways of getting on with each other. Like any other learning process, the responsibility for change lies with you. If you are to make proper use of this advice, you will need to make a special joint effort to follow all the suggestions. You will need to set aside time to be together—time to talk to each other without frequent interruptions from children or whatever. Try to find a regular half-hour (or longer) in the day that is exclusively for you.

You will also need to aim for at least three sessions a week of physical contact—although, of course, the more spontaneous and natural these occasions are, the better. You will need privacy (a lock on the bedroom door is not anti-social) and comfort. If sound-proofing is a problem, put the radio on. Going to bed earlier is the easiest way to find time for the sessions. A drink around bedtime may help;

several drinks won't. Don't expect miracles at first. You may even
have to force yourself to practise to begin with. This is not surprising
if you have been 'off' sex for quite a time; you will need to unlearn all
your old habits and attitudes, wipe the slate clean, and allow your
natural feelings to re-emerge—that is, if you want them to. Even if you
are keen to have a baby, it is much wiser to delay getting pregnant
until after you have had a chance of improving your sexual
relationship. Therefore, I advise you to use an effective method of
contraception whilst following this advice.

I suggest that you and your partner read the notes that follow, and
decide *independently* whether you want to work on improving your
sexual relationship now, and whether you are prepared to make the
full commitment in terms of setting aside time, making an effort, and
accepting the agreed limits on your physical relationship for a short
time.

To start with I will be suggesting definite limits beyond which you
should not go in a lovemaking session. At first this may seem a bit
clinical, as though you were making love to doctor's orders, but this is
a temporary phase. Before long you should be able to set yourselves
limits when making love—to be able to say 'stop' without fearing that
your partner will feel upset, angry or rejected. Only when you feel safe
enough to stop will you really enjoy going on.

*Stage I: touching your partner for your own pleasure without genital
contact*

This stage of the programme emphasises the importance of keeping
safe within limits. A formal agreement must be made between you to
ban all attempts at intercourse or genital contact until you feel
comfortable with these early stages of the programme. This puts
implicit trust in each partner to abide by the agreement, and any
attempt to sabotage the trust should be taken very seriously. This ban
is essential if performance anxiety is to be reduced. It removes any
particular goal, reduces the pressure in you to succeed, allows you to
experience new feelings, and lets physical contact become an end in
itself.

You should aim for two or three sessions a week; take it in turns to
start a session (don't leave it to the man). Each session has two parts.
If you touch him first, touch him the way *you* want to (his job is to

relax and stop you doing things he doesn't like); then in the same session, he touches you the way *he* likes (your job is to relax and protect yourself from discomfort). Do it separately; it slows everything down, and helps you to learn to relax (once you have overcome your embarrassment, that is).

Important points to remember.
If you are doing the caressing—assert yourself. Touch your partner where *you* want to touch (anywhere on the body except the genital area and breasts) in a way that is nice for you and for as long as you wish. Experiment and touch parts of the body you have not touched before, using your hands, or mouth, or any other part of your body.

If you are being caressed—relax. Protect yourself if you don't like what is being done to you (the easiest way to do this is to move your partner's hand elsewhere, or say 'stop'). You will need to recognise if and when you are 'spectatoring'—which means watching your body being touched rather than participating fully by feeling the sensations that you are experiencing. Don't worry if this happens at first; you must learn to realise when you are doing it and learn ways to get out of it. There are two things to do—(a) concentrate on relaxing your whole body and concentrate in addition on the sensations produced by your partner; (b) stop caressing for a short time until you feel sufficiently relaxed and ready to start again.

It is nice to touch and feel close to your partner.

It is nice to be touched.

Aim for three sessions a week taking it in turns to initiate the sessions with the initiator caressing first. You may have to push yourself into starting a session, feeling little motivation or drive to begin. This is a common experience, partly because of the artificiality of the situation, partly because people feel a little embarrassed and awkward at first (perhaps because of longstanding resistance to body contact from previous experiences that have gone wrong). It is important to see this stage as a stepping-stone towards a spontaneous sexual relationship.
Some people find this stage pleasantly relaxing; others find it arousing. It doesn't matter which, but it is important for you to recognise what you are feeling. If, after the session, you find yourself

very aroused and unable to settle, it is quite permissible to relieve your tension by masturbating—but it should be done by you, not your partner. If you are quite clear about these limits you will probably find that this relief of tension is not necessary.

Problems and Snags. If you or your partner cannot bring yourself to try this limited sort of touching—or find the whole idea silly or repulsive—you should stop and ask yourself seriously what is holding you back from such a simple exchange. Usually, it will turn out to be some grudge you are feeling towards the other person, in which case you need to try talking about it; or perhaps it is anxiety, depression or guilt feelings within yourself. Look again at the causes of sexual problems, or re-read Chapter 3 or 5 (whichever is relevant for you).

Until you have tackled the underlying difficulties you will not *want* to caress each other, and the whole exercise will seem futile, boring or a waste of time. That only demonstrates that the whole purpose of sexual contact for you is to reach a physical climax, whereas in the context of a relationship it ought to be a mutually pleasing exchange of physical contact—which is what these sessions are designed to promote.

Stage II: providing 'feedback' while being touched

In addition to touching each other, in whatever way you choose to, you should now ask for feedback from your partner, and show him or her what *you* like too; this is good sexual communication! Try it—however long you have been together! Praise and encourage the things that you like, either in words or with grunts or by putting your partner's hand back for more. (Don't take over complete control though; that's your partner's responsibility). If something could be even nicer, put your hand on your partner's to demonstrate how you would like it (harder, softer, faster, slower, more to the left, etc.); then leave it to your partner. In this way the person caressing still maintains complete control, but the person being caressed is beginning to give some feedback as to what is especially nice for him or her. But remember, it is up to the person caressing to choose what he or she does. Remember to discuss with each other how you felt after each session— 'self-assert' and 'self-protect'. Remember that it's nice to see your partner enjoy being touched by you.

Stage III: touching with genital contact

Exactly the same basic principles apply for this stage of the programme. A ban on intercourse persists, but now genital contact with the hands and/or mouth is permitted.

Each session is in two parts as before: A caressing B and then B caressing A. As before, alternate partners initiate the session, each touching in the way he or she wants to touch, with the partner protecting himself or herself from hurt and guiding the hand to show what is particularly pleasurable. When genital contact occurs, subtle changes in pressure, speed or direction can have profound effects on the sensation received, so it is even more important to be able to communicate what is best for you—and remember, it will not be the same for each session. Your body sensitivity can vary from day to day.

Do not concentrate solely on the genital regions; spend as much time as before on general body caressing and kissing as well. The use of body lotions or KY jelly can enhance the pleasure for both of you, especially when touching genital areas. The only goal is to be able to relax and enjoy what is happening. Check for 'spectating', and learn ways of getting back to being fully relaxed and involved. The partner being caressed may or may not become aroused, and may or may not ejaculate or reach a climax. The response will vary from session to session—that is normal. Do not aim for climax or orgasm; but if it does occur it does not matter, and need not mean the end of a session.

Stage IV (page 103) will be considered after looking at special techniques which may be necessary at this stage.

Special techniques

Problems with erections. As with all sexual problems, a man must deal with the background causes if he is to tackle his problems with erections. During Stage III he should encourage his partner to caress his penis in a way that he enjoys; or he can caress it himself, concentrating on relaxing his body and focusing on his genital sensations. Use KY jelly to help in lubrication when doing the caressing. It is good to be able to allow an erection to come and go and come and go—this gives confidence that it will return, and that a fading erection need not signal a panic attack. The more you relax, the more your body will function normally. Make no attempt to have intercourse in the early sessions, even if you have a full erection—you will avoid the demands of a 'performance' that way.

Problems with a woman's response.   Exactly the same principles apply as above. A woman should encourage her partner—by holding his fingers—to caress her outer genitalia and clitoris in a way that feels nice for her, concentrating on relaxing and feeling the resultant sensations. She should *not* aim for intercourse, even if aroused, and should allow the arousal to come and go. If either of you feels tense, you should stop for a minute or two then start again.

Problems with orgasm.   Orgasms only occur if you feel relaxed and want them to happen in that particular setting. Many women go through their lives without experiencing orgasm, and still enjoy their sexual experiences. An orgasm is like a sneeze—sexual and muscle tension builds up until a reflex trigger occurs, which sets off the sudden release of muscle tension, often associated with an extra burst of heightened sensation and body awareness. Some women find their orgasm uncomfortable on occasions, which may be associated with contractions of their uterus or womb.

If a woman has never experienced orgasm, she should try the limited caressing steps and when sexually aroused, using KY jelly as a lubricant, caress her own clitoris (the small knob of tissue at the front of the vagina) with her own or her partner's fingers, concentrating her attention on relaxing her body and at the same time focusing on the sensations she is receiving from the stimulation. Many women fear that an orgasm will be a 'catastrophic event', and frighten themselves off as they feel their sexual tension mounting. They should gradually increase the time of stimulation until they have reassured themselves that nothing alarming is going to happen (in fact the whole event may feel like an anticlimax in the end!). Some women learn to experience their first orgasm using a vibrator, then progress to accepting their partner's caressing in a more relaxed way once they have acquired the experience and confidence that they can achieve orgasm.

If you continue to have problems reaching climax, look again at the background causes of sexual problems; are you sure you are not feeling angry or insecure with your partner or yourself? If you are, discuss your feelings with each other.

A Self-Help Approach to Sexual Problems

Premature ejaculation. This problem can be first tackled during Stage III (the 'genital caressing' stage of the programme). Every man has a point of no return after which he cannot avoid ejaculation. During your partner's caressing of your penis, you may feel yourself getting aroused to such a degree that you can predict that you will ejaculate shortly.

You must aim to stop your partner's caresses at a stage just short of the point of no return and allow your arousal level to subside slightly (say for half a minute), and then return to being caressed and repeat the process of stopping when you again feel near the point of inevitable ejaculation again. The difficulty at first is knowing when to ask your partner to stop. This is a learning process which every male has to undertake at some stage in his life and it is never too late to learn control of ejaculation. It will, however, take time and practice and will require the understanding and co-operation of your partner. Once your anxiety level begins to fall and your confidence builds up, you should find an increasing ability to control your ejaculation, and once a slight improvement occurs your confidence will increase and so will your control.

If you have difficulty in gaining control using this method (remember, it will take time, because you are changing what is probably a long-established pattern) then you can try the 'squeeze technique': just before the point of no return, you stop stimulation of the penis and either you or your partner grasp the tip of the penis between fingers and thumb at the point of attachment of the foreskin and squeeze firmly for ten seconds or so. This reduces the reflex ejaculation response (and possibly the erection too) in the same way that biting your lip stops a sneeze. You can then resume stimulation and repeat the process if necessary.

Both the stop-start and squeeze technique are effective in delaying ejaculation during manual stimulation of the penis or during sexual intercourse at a later stage in the programme.

Delayed ejaculation. If a man has never been able to ejaculate successfully inside his partner's vagina, he should learn—by caressing or strong self-stimulation (or by the use of a vibrator)—to become aroused and ejaculate close to his partner, and gradually move closer and closer to her until he can move his penis onto and into her body. If such an approach fails, he should ask for referral to a sexual problems clinic or to a psychologist who may be able to help release his deep-seated inhibitions, which will usually be the cause.

Vaginismus. This condition is different from the other sexual problems because a woman who does not permit penetration of her vagina by her partner's penis or finger may still enjoy sexual stimulation and respond normally. Vaginismus may be caused by two main conditions—fear of pain or fear of growing up. Some women fear pain with intercourse because they have grown up believing it will hurt (this anxiety perhaps fanned by stories from their mother or other significant people in their lives); or they may have had an unpleasant experience involving their genitalia in the past—they may have been sexually assaulted in childhood, suffered a painful vaginal examination, had an unwanted pregnancy, or been hurt accidentally. Such a woman becomes programmed to believe that vaginal contact will cause pain and of course, if the vaginal muscles are in spasm when penetration is attempted, this will indeed confirm her own worst suspicions as the tense muscles are painfully stretched against her will.

Such a woman should teach herself to be relaxed—by exercises to relax her whole body—before she attempts any form of vaginal penetration; and she should learn to tighten and relax her vaginal muscles (the same muscles that stop you passing water in mid-flow). With her vaginal muscles relaxed, and with plenty of KY jelly on her finger, she should try to insert her own or her partner's finger into her vagina. If she decides to use his finger, he should promise to leave all control to her. Once the finger is inside she should leave it there for three minutes at least, and practise tightening and relaxing her vaginal muscles until she is confident that she feels no pain with the finger in position. (Remember that a vagina can stretch enormously provided that the muscles are relaxed.) Once she can accept two fingers comfortably she should then attempt the Stage IV instructions. In rare cases there may be a physical obstruction to the vaginal opening, and if this is suspected, she should seek medical advice.

If a woman feels an extremely strong reluctance to contemplate the possibility of consummating the relationship, she should ask herself whether this represents a disinclination to become deeply involved in her relationship with this man. It may be that she is undecided about her commitment to him, or—more commonly—undecided about her commitment to growing up and leaving her virginal state. Each woman must make her own private choice on this matter, and if she has chosen to remain virginal she should declare this to her partner. Many relationships survive happily without full intercourse, but of course remain infertile. Such couples can cause the medical profession quite a headache if they demand artificial insemination to achieve a pregnancy. Ask yourself what you would do if faced with such a request. It confronts us with some basic questions about the role of an active sex life in our day-to-day existence, and its significance to our overall adjustment to life.

Stage IV: 'inviting' the penis into the vagina

Once caressing and genital contact is going well, if the male partner is getting reasonably firm erections then you are ready to enter this stage of the programme. As before, this stage is designed to allow the freedom to experience sensations of physical contact with each other without performance anxiety (fear of failing to achieve a particular goal).

After a period of mutual caressing involving the genital area, when you (the woman) feel that you are ready, and when you feel your partner has a reasonably firm erection, you invite the penis into your vagina. The easiest position is the 'female superior'. In this position the man lies flat on his back. The woman kneels above him with her knees on either side of his body more or less at the level of his nipples. In this position she is well placed, by lowering her bottom, to guide and insert his penis into her vagina. This means that the woman keeps full control over what is happening. The aim of this stage is to re-acquaint yourselves with the body sensation of a penis in a vagina. The woman should tighten and relax her vaginal muscles on the penis, which she may or may not be able to feel once it is inside the vagina. The penis itself is receiving little direct stimulation from this static position, and the man may well find his erection gets less. If you wish, you can then resume genital caressing and perhaps repeat the process over again. Remember that you are both to concentrate on the sensations you are feeling from your genital region and relax, and not to start any thrusting movements. Initially you should only allow vaginal containment for a brief period. The period of containment can be gradually lengthened in each session.

After a period of vaginal containment, you may try some limited thrusting movements to see how this affects your sensations. Only do this briefly to start with, but if you are both enjoying the feelings this produces, allow the movements to continue.

Even at this stage, it is essential that either of you can say 'stop' at any time. In this way you avoid the feeling that once vaginal 'intercourse' has started you have to go on regardless. You are setting the limits for yourselves now. Practise this by saying 'stop'. Remember that, even if you are enjoying lovemaking, your partner may want to stop and needs to be able to without fear that you will get angry. This is what a secure, safe sexual relationship is about—and when you feel really safe you'll usually want to carry on.

The movements of intercourse feel different in the different positions you can try and it is important to experiment to find ways that suit you both. You may find one position nicer for one of you and another position better for the other.

Your responsiveness will vary from session to session and at different times of the month. This is normal for both sexes. Many women have slightly less lubrication and are less likely to reach a climax just before a period, but this is not always the case. Many women enjoy clitoral stimulation in addition to the thrusting of the penis, and most find that they reach a climax most comfortably and pleasurably in this manner. This is normal and not a sign that they are not fully aroused. Many women can also have a highly satisfactory and highly aroused sexual experience without a climax. It is an important rule to remember that provided physical contact is enjoyable, an orgasm is not necessary. It is also a myth that a joint climax is the ideal. Most people find it very pleasurable to enjoy the experience of their partner's climax, separate from their own, whilst on occasions they may enjoy coming together. These are all variations on the theme of making love and what you enjoy will depend on your feelings and the state of mind at the time. The only goal is to enjoy yourselves—together.

In conclusion, if after trying this self-help approach to your sexual problems you have not progressed, then I would suggest that you ask your family doctor to refer you to the nearest psychosexual clinic—the address of the Directory of Sexual Advisory Services is in the Appendix. It is not uncommon for sexual and marital problems to be so complex that a counsellor is necessary to unravel and defuse the tensions and conflicts that exist between a couple. Nevertheless, I hope that the contents of this book will have increased your understanding of the pleasures and pitfalls of everyday sexual relationships, so that you can tolerate or enjoy more comfortably your own state of affairs, whether alone or with another.

Good luck!

Useful Addresses and Further Reading

Association of Sexual and Marital Therapists, P.O. Box 62, Sheffield S10 3TS

Directory of Sexual Advisory Services, 42 Fulready Road, London E10 6DU

National Marriage Guidance Council, Herbert Gray College, 1 Little Church Street, Rugby *(local office in your telephone directory)*

Brook Advisory Centres (Central Office), 153A East Street, Walworth, London SE17 2DS
(local office in your telephone directory)

Institute of Psychosexual Medicine, 10 Peterswood Hill, Ware, Herts.

Sexual and Personal Relationships of the Disabled, 49 Brook House, Torrington Place, London WC1

Albany Trust (for sexual minority groups), 16-18 Stratton Ground, London SW1 2HP

Campaign for Homosexual Equality, 274 Upper Street, Islington, London N1 2UA

Scottish Homosexual Rights Group, 60 Broughton Street, Edinburgh

Beaumont Society (for transvestites), B.M., P.O. Box 3084, London WC1N 3XX

Self-Help Association for Transsexuals, 4 Adelaide Square, Windsor, Berks W19 9SB

Rape Crisis Centre, P.O. Box 42, London N6 5BU

The Joy of Sex	A. Comfort; Quartet Books (1975)
The Book of Love	D. Devlin; New English Library (1974)
Sex Manners for Men	R. Charthan; New English Library (1980)
Becoming Orgasmic	J. Heimen & J. Piccolo; Prentice Hall, New York (1976)
How a baby is made	(for children) P. H. Knudsen; Pan Books (1973)